D0833939

Birds of Prey
of Britain and Europe

A CONCISE GUIDE IN COLOUR

Birds of Prey
of Britain and Europe

by
Dr Miroslav Bouchner
Illustrated by
Dan Bárta
Consultant Editor
D. M. Broom MA PhD

HAMLYN
LONDON • NEW YORK • SYDNEY • TORONTO

Translated by Olga Kuthanová

Designed and produced by Artia for
The Hamlyn Publishing Group Limited
London ● New York ● Sydney ● Toronto
Astronaut House, Feltham, Middlesex, England

ISBN 600 31291 7

Printed in Czechoslovakia
3/02/23/51-01

CONTENTS

FOREWORD

One of many human traits is the desire to measure values. In practically every situation, a person asks himself the question of what value a given thing has for him, whether it will pay to do this or that, what is to his advantage, and what is not. This trait naturally asserts itself also in his relation to animals. Believing that the world was created only for him, man designated animals as either useful or harmful according to whether the given creature was of benefit to him or not. Animals that feed on meat are anathema to him, even though they are to a great extent useful in various ways. Therefore, man often proclaims, in typically human fashion, that raptors and owls, for instance, are shameless and cruel thieves, entirely forgetting that they can live solely by this means and many of their anatomical features are adapted to hunting live prey. Very often even anthropomorphizes them. Cunning and cruelty, for example, which man popularly attributes not only to birds of prey but to other carnivorous animals as well, are really intelligible to man only as human characteristics.

It is hard to say when man first began to classify animals in this human fashion. It was probably when, thanks to his intellect, he began to gain superiority over other animals, for whom he had hitherto served as prey, and when he began to realize that beasts of prey, raptors, owls, and other carnivorous animals were his rivals in that they hunted the same animals he hunted for food.

Nowadays we try to judge the behaviour of raptors and beasts of prey objectively because they are a necessary and important part of the balance of nature but we still cannot rid ourselves of the deeply rooted comparison of values.

The farmer considers the Kestrel and Buzzard useful raptors because they catch fieldmice, ground squirrels and hamsters. Likewise the Sparrowhawk, because it catches large numbers of House Sparrows, which sometimes feed on grain crops. The gamekeeper, on the other hand, would kill these raptors on sight because they might also kill a chick of a pheasant or partridge.

Man does not mind in the least if in the wild some animal hunts creatures he himself has no use for. Woe betide, however, if it captures an animal man considers his exclusive property. It does not matter if, for example, a stork feeds on frogs, lizards, or reptiles which many people consider useful. Great, however, will be the hue and cry if, in periods of drought when pools dry up and frogs are scarce, the same bird captures a small pheasant chick, though the neighbourhood is full of them. Man is upset because he lays claim to this bird and because the stork has deprived him of a tasty dish of wildfowl.

Now let us look at the problem from another angle. There is no doubt that under certain circumstances pheasants, hares, or deer can do much damage to young forest stands as well as farm crops. In such a case, however, they are usually pardoned because in the autumn they make up for the damage by providing man with delicious meat. The two examples are practically identical: pheasants and deer cause damage only on occasion, the same as the Buzzard or Kestrel captures a partridge only on occasion. The conclusions drawn from these facts, however, differ, the decisive factor in determining harmfulness or usefulness in each case being its direct benefit to man. In the first instance, the compensation for damage caused by pheasants or other wild game is tangible and immediately evident, whereas it is quite difficult to visualize the benefits yielded by a Buzzard, Kestrel, owl or Stoat, and these are never properly appreciated. That is also one of the reasons why many hunters the world over shoot raptors and owls throughout the year regardless of the limits of the hunting season or the prohibition to hunt.

Another of man's traits is that he is always on the side of the victim, never stopping to consider that the animal in question is often very plentiful and in numerous instances capable of breeding rapidly, so that the loss of a single individual is not at all detrimental to the population as a whole. Falcons, eagles, kites, harriers, and other raptors, however, have been completely exterminated by man in places or else have been driven into the remotest parts of the world by the inroads of civilization.

The progress of civilization with all its accompanying negative factors has a detrimental effect on nature as a whole. Behind it all, however, is man; all this is the result of his activity. Thankfully, people are beginning to realize the danger which threatens all living things including man himself. As things stand, the protection of the environment as a whole is becoming man's primary task. Everybody can do his bit to prevent the irresponsible destruction of the natural environment and to make the protection of rare animal species, which include owls and raptors, the object of general concern. Hunters must realize the power they have over nature when they hold a gun in their hands and they should know when to and when not to shoot — that is the aim of this book. Its purpose is the conservation of nature, the gift of several more years of life to the already endangered and greatly decimated groups of owls and raptors.

RAPTORS

Structure of a raptor's body

The term raptor is often used in approximately the same sense as bird of prey to mean a species that hunts and kills other animals for food. In this book, the term raptor is taken to mean any bird of the order Falconiformes; owls are treated separately. It should be remembered that members of the Falconiformes may be referred to as diurnal raptors (that is, hunting mainly by day) and owls as nocturnal raptors (that is, hunting mainly by night).

Books on ornithology usually state that raptors are medium-large to large birds. When we consider, however, that there are some 8600 bird species throughout the world, that the smallest hummingbird is about the same size and weight as a bumblebee, and that the largest and heaviest birds — Ostriches — may weigh as much as 150 kilograms, then it is difficult to decide where lies the dividing line between small, medium-large, and large birds. This division proves unsatisfactory even within the order of raptors, which apart from the arctic and antarctic, have a worldwide distribution and number 267 species divided among 89 genera. Therefore, this book will avoid possible confusion by stating dimensions and weight and/or comparing the given bird with other, commonly known birds.

New World and Old World vultures, the largest birds of prey, attain truly formidable dimensions and are among the largest and heaviest of living birds capable of flight (the Ostrich lost its powers of flight as a result of its way of life). The great Andean Condor weighs about 11 kilograms and has a wingspan of as much as 3.5 metres (certain older individuals). Found in Pleistocene deposits in California were the remains of *Teratornis incredibilis,* a vulture with a wingspan of about 5 metres and weight of more than 20 kilograms. Few flying birds weigh more than the Andean Condor, except, for example, the Mute Swan and Great Bustard and only the Wandering Albatross has a greater wingspan. Old World vultures attain dimensions that are only slightly smaller; many weigh as much as 7 kilograms and have a wingspan of more than 2.5 metres.

On the other hand, the smallest raptors, found in Asia, are even somewhat smaller than the Starling and weigh about 45 grams. One of the smallest European raptors is the Lesser Kestrel, which weighs 150 to 200 grams, measures 30 to 35 centimetres in length, and has a wingspan of 65 to 75 centimetres; in other words, it is only slightly larger than the Turtle Dove. Medium-large raptors have a wingspan of 120 to 150 centimetres and weigh 800 to 1000 grams.

In many birds of prey, there are marked differences in size between the sexes. The female is generally larger than the male and in some cases the difference is so great that the layman might think the male, which has a somewhat dissimilar coloration and may often weigh as much as a third less, belongs to an entirely different species. Such differences, known as sexual dimorphism, may be found, for example, in the falcons, Sparrowhawk, and Goshawk.

Their superficial similarities make raptors a fairly uniform group so that even a layman can recognize them as birds of prey at first glance. A typical characteristic of the entire order is the strong, often massive bill, down-curved at the tip, the sharp edges of the upper mandible overlapping the lower mandible. It is somewhat compressed and always higher than wide. Only rarely does the upper mandible have a straight edge; in most instances it is slightly curved and in some species (falcons) it has a sharp notch called

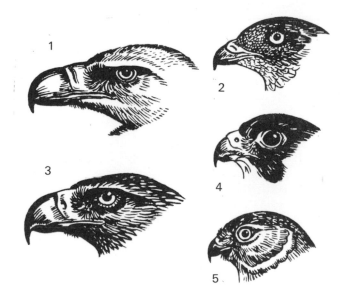

Fig. 1   Various raptors' bills
1 Griffon Vulture   2 Honey Buzzard   3 Golden Eagle   4 Peregrine Falcon   5 Pallid Harrier (female)
The bills of vultures and eagles are strong and can easily handle even large prey. In the Honey Buzzard the space at the base of the bill is covered with stiff feathers which protect it from the stings of wasps. The bill of falcons has a pronounced 'tooth'. Harriers have a facial disc resembling that of owls.

a tooth. Shrikes have similar bills, but these are much smaller birds belonging to an entirely different order — the Passeriformes. Some raptors have two such teeth, which make it easier for the bird to hold the prey and tear the flesh. This, of course, does not mean that raptors without a tooth have greater difficulty tearing meat. All birds of prey have very strong bills and can manage to handle even very tough food. The base of the upper bill is covered with a leathery cere, which is usually coloured yellow or greyish blue.

A further characteristic of birds of prey, closely linked with their method of procuring food, is the long-toed, clawed foot. All raptors have four toes; one turned backward and the other three pointing forward. Only the Osprey has a reversible outer toe, the same as owls, cuckoos, and woodpeckers. The undersides of the toes are covered with horny pads or spines which serve to maintain a secure hold on the prey — this is a useful adaptation for fish eating. Raptors which hunt live prey have strongly hooked talons, the ones on the first and second toes being generally stronger and slightly hollowed out below, forming sharp edges on either side that make for easier penetration into the victim's body. Raptors that do not hunt live prey but feed solely on carrion have fairly short, blunt talons. The feet of vultures are not adapted for catching or grasping prey but only for running on the ground. Other raptors not only capture but also kill their prey with their feet and use

Fig. 2 Various raptors' feet
1 Honey Buzzard   2 Goshawk   3 Golden Eagle   4 White-tailed Eagle
5 Peregrine Falcon   6 Osprey   7 Lammergeier
The toes and talons are adapted for catching all kinds of prey. The Goshawk, Golden Eagle, White-tailed Eagle, and Peregrine Falcon have

long toes with long, narrow talons. The undersides of the Osprey's toes are covered with horny pads to maintain a firm hold on the slippery fishes it feeds on. The toes of the Honey Buzzard and vultures are short and the talons relatively blunt because they are not used to hunt prey.

them to hold the victim while devouring the meat. They have enormous strength in the toes, the force of their grasp being augmented by a special arrangement of the tendons. When the bird alights on its victim, the tendons automatically contract, the toes draw together, and the victim has practically no hope of escape.

The raptor's body is covered with largely stiff, closely fitting feathers. The wing quills and tail feathers are particularly stiff and are of importance for the various forms of flight. The toes, tarsus (in most species), cere, eye ring, and gape are bare. Some food specialists that feed only on the carcasses of large animals (vultures) have the head and part of the neck entirely bare or covered only with short down feathers. The plumage is coloured various shades of black, grey, brown, and white. Individuals of the same species may be variable in colour. In many instances the coloration of juvenile birds differs from that of the adults (Goshawk, Sea Eagle), in others the male's plumage differs from that of the female (Kestrel, harriers), and in some species, where the young and mature birds as well as the male and female are alike, there is such variability in coloration that practically no two individuals are identical (Common Buzzard and Rough-legged Buzzard). The bare patches of skin — toes, tarsus, cere, eye ring — are generally coloured yellow, grey, or bluish.

The short contour feathers are rounded at the tips, only in some cases are they pointed (in eagles on the nape and hind neck). At the base of the bill and on the lores, that is, the space between the eye and the bill, the feathers are in the form of bristles. In the Honey Buzzard this space is covered with stiff feathers arranged like scales which serve to protect it from the stings of the wasps and hornets it feeds on. The feathers on the legs are longer and form so-called 'pantaloons'. The wings are often long and powerful. Some raptors (falcons) have fairly narrow wings with pointed tips and quills close together; others (eagles, vultures) have long, broad wings with quills spread apart

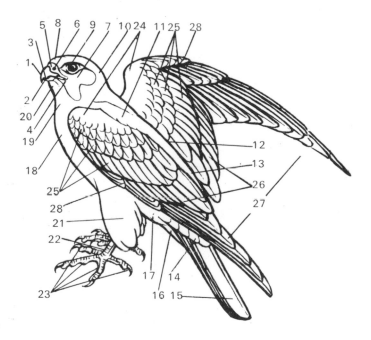

Fig. 3   The exterior features of the bird
1 upper mandible 2 lower mandible 3 tooth 4 lores 5 cere
6 nostril 7 ear coverts 8 forehead 9 crown 10 nape 11 mantle
12 back 13 rump 14 upper tail coverts 15 tail 16 under tail
coverts 17 belly 18 breast 19 throat 20 chin 21 tibial
feathers (pantaloons) 22 tarsus 23 toes 24 carpus 25 wing
coverts 26 secondaries 27 primaries 28 bastard wing.

like fingers, and still others (Goshawk, Sparrowhawk) have short, broad wings that are rounded at the tip. The shape of the wings and the arrangement of the quills are directly related to the method of flight and the way the birds seek their food.

The tarsus is covered with horny scales. The claws, toes, and tarsus comprise the bird's most important implement in hunting prey and, because the victim often defends itself in all sorts of ways, this armour is most expedient and necessary. The length of the toes and the tarsus is always related to the type of prey the bird feeds on and the method by which it procures its food.

Raptors are very strong for their size. The skeleton is sturdy and massive and the large bones are to a marked extent pneumatic. Hollow bones with air sacs extending into them have greater strength per unit weight than solid bones would have (hollow bones and pneumatization bones, however, are not restricted to raptors but may be found in other birds as well). Attached to the high keel of the fairly large, broad breast bone are the powerful flight muscles. Raptors generally alight on elevated spots in an upright position, and in this position the large, broad breast can clearly be seen.

The egg

The male reproductive organ consists of paired testes located next to the kidneys. Some time before mating, the testes begin to enlarge until they are several times their original size. The mature male gametes pass through the two seminal ducts to the cloaca, from where they pass into the female's body during copulation. The ovary of the female is shaped like a cluster of grapes. Outside the breeding period, it is very small and located above the upper edge of the kidneys. In most female birds, only the left ovary is fully developed; the right one is usually rudimentary. In birds of prey and certain other species, however, the right ovary may also function.

At the start of the breeding period the ovary begins to increase in size until it is so large that the individual eggs are visible to the naked eye. When mature, the eggs fall off from the cluster into the long oviduct where they are fertilized by the sperm and where they acquire further membranes. When it falls into the oviduct, the egg consists only of the yolk, acquiring several layers of egg white, two paper-thin membranes, and finally a hard, calcareous shell during its passage through the duct. The shell is formed in the uterus, which is a continuation of the oviduct. There it also acquires variously coloured markings such as streaks, spots, blotches, and so on. The colour forms in the separate layers of the calcium carbonate and is not laid on when the shell is complete. This explains why some spots on a raptor's egg are dull and not very distinct because they are deep inside the shell, whereas others are clear and distinct where the pigment is either just below the surface or directly on the outside of the shell. The colouring of the shell is produced by two pigments: oocyan, derived from bile pigment, which produces green and blue tints; and protoporphyrin, derived from haemoglobin, which produces brownish-red tints. The completed egg then passes from the uterus through the narrow vagina to the cloaca.

Raptors' eggs are generally short and elliptical. The eggs of some owls, on the other hand, are almost spherical though they may also be short and oval. Those of some birds, such as many owls, are white, others are more or less spotted or speckled, in various shades of the colours mentioned above.

The elaborate organs for breathing

Compared with the musical notes of songbirds, the calls of raptors are not particularly attractive. Most utter sharp sounds reminiscent of woodpeckers, others utter high, barking, rapidly repeated notes. The range includes mewing calls, hoarse cries, whistling notes as well as sounds resembling laughter. Only a few raptors have voices that are pleasant to the ear. They are most vocal during the courting period.

Just behind the tongue there is a narrow opening into the larynx, which is formed by a continuous succession of cartilaginous rings. This is where the vocal organs of mammals — the vocal chords — are usually located. Birds, however, produce sounds by means of the syrinx, a special organ not present in mammals, which is located at the point where the trachea branches into the bronchial tubes. Here, the passage formed by cartilaginous rings widens to form a space partitioned off by a horizontal band. Between this and the wall of the syrinx stretch the vocal membranes which are governed by special muscles and made to vibrate by the current of air passing through as the bird inhales and exhales thereby producing sounds.

The lungs of raptors, like those of other birds, are sponge-like, small, compact, motionless organs held in the chest cavity by special ligament. Birds lack a diaphragm like that of mammals so that when they are at rest, air is inhaled and exhaled by the action of muscles which move the breast bone changing the size of the thoracic cavity, and also by the muscles which change the volume of the various air sacs.

The bronchial tubes do not open into the lungs as they do in mammals but pass through them and terminate in five pairs of large, thin-walled air sacs, several times larger in volume than the lungs themselves. These cavities are greatly branched so that they reach various parts of the body, provide the pneumatic filling of the hollow bones, and penetrate between the layers of muscles.

Air sacs enable the bird to breathe in the way necessary for a physically tiring activity such as flying or diving. In powered flight, effected by beating the wings, or rapid headlong dives, when the speed of an attacking raptor often exceeds 100 kilometres an hour, the breast muscles are fully engaged and normal breathing by means of the expansion and contraction of the chest cavity is either totally impossible or greatly limited. During the upward stroke of the wings, air passes through the lungs into the air sacs, filling them completely. Then, during the downward stroke of the wings, the air sacs are compressed and the air is expelled through the lungs and out through the bill. Thus, all the oxygen taken from the air and the blood is oxygenated when the air is inhaled and when it is exhaled. The faster the bird flaps its wings the quicker the air 'pump' works and the greater the supply of oxygen to the blood.

Furthermore, air sacs play an important role in regulating the body temperature. They not only serve to lead off excess heat but also to insulate the body, particularly the underside, against cold.

Air sacs also serve a purely mechanical purpose. In

the pursuit of prey, and especially in headlong dives when a falcon, for instance, is capable of attaining a speed of perhaps 250 kilometres an hour within a few seconds, the air sacs serve to cushion vital internal organs and keep them in the same position. During sudden, abrupt changes in speed they prevent undesirable movements of the heart, stomach, liver, windpipe, and alimentary canal.

Keenness of sight

Eyesight is very important in the hunting activity of a bird of prey. If we were to chart an attack by a raptor in stages according to the parts of the body involved in each successive stage it would be as follows: eyes, wings, claws, bill. The prey is sighted with the eyes, overtaken with the aid of the wings, seized with the claws and killed (sometimes, in falcons for example, with the aid of the bill), and eaten with the bill. That is why birds of prey have large eyes which, unlike those of other birds, are turned slightly forward giving a wide field of binocular vision. In raptors, such as falcons, that hunt their prey in the air, the eyes are located at the sides of the head and protrude somewhat like two periscopes, affording a wide field of vision. In raptors that hunt their prey on the ground, among trees, or in thickets, and capture their prey by a sudden, unexpected attack (some eagles, Sparrowhawk, Goshawk) the eyes are turned more towards the front and are topped by massive arches. Such eyes focus on the space in front of the bird and on the ground below and block out extraneous, disrupting factors that are of no importance to the bird. The iris of a raptor's eye is generally coloured yellow, orange-yellow, brown, or grey.

All birds, and raptors in particular, have exceptionally keen eyesight, perhaps the best of all animals. What takes the human eye several repeated and searching glances to register clearly and in detail, takes a bird no more than an instant.

The term used in judging the efficiency of an eye is 'acuity of vision' — the ability to distinguish the smallest detail in a given plane. Various experiments and calculations have shown that visual types of animals (including man, monkeys, and birds) have the best visual acuity. A dog may see a moving target as much as 250 metres distant. A falcon is able to see a perching dove as much as 1000 metres away and a flying dove more than 1600 metres distant. At a distance of 100 metres, if the light conditions are good, the human eye can see a surface 1.65 centimetres in diameter, a cat a surface 7.8 centimetres in diameter, a Red Deer a surface 15.5 centimetres in diameter, and a Brown Rat is unable to distinguish a surface smaller than 75.6 centimetres in diameter. Raptors have far greater visual acuity. At a distance of 100 metres, an eagle is able to distinguish a surface 0.47 centimetres in diameter. The Common Buzzard, for example, sees as clearly and as far as a man does using a field glass with seven- to eight-fold magnification. When these figures are calculated in terms of the size of the prey raptors hunt, then an eagle can sight a mouse or fieldmouse from a height of 1 kilometre in good light. These statistics were calculated from the results of experiments with birds of prey and other animals in captivity. Besides, birds do not need to continually adjust the focal length of the eye as man does. An eagle sees a victim or enemy some distance away just as clearly as something lying at its feet. I remember, for instance, the visual acuity of a Kestrel I kept in captivity. It was perching on the floor in a large room when suddenly it ran to the corner about 8 metres away and, with its bill, grasped a centipede about 2 centimetres long. I should never have been able to perceive such a tiny creature, let alone at such an oblique angle.

Sight, then, is the most important of the senses of diurnal birds of prey. The others are not nearly as perfect, even though the sense of hearing is fairly well developed, too. Owls have exceptional hearing. This is understandable, because, in daytime, hearing is not as important as eyesight in procuring food and perceiving danger.

Most books on ornithology state that the sense of smell is practically non-existent in birds. Apart from New Zealand's kiwis and many seabirds, however, which have a truly keen sense of smell, the American vultures are also birds with a good sense of smell. Some were able to find food concealed by an opaque cover or in hardly accessible places. Vultures of the virgin forests, where eyesight is not of much use in locating carrion in the dense vegetation, are also birds that have demonstrated that they possess a good olfactory sense.

Feeding and hunting methods of raptors

Birds of prey consume large quantities of food with long intervals between meals, and the digestive system is adapted accordingly. As a rule, smaller species consume more food in relation to their size than large species. For example, the Kestrel, which weighs about 180 grams in the case of the male and 213 grams in the case of the female, consumes daily about 50 grams of food (the equivalent of two to three adult fieldmice), in other words, 23 to 27 per cent of its body weight. The Imperial Eagle weighs 3.5 to 4 kilograms and consumes an average of 500 grams of meat daily, only 11 to 14 per cent of the bird's body weight. Raptors need to eat large quantities of food to supply the great deal of energy that they expend.

Raptors do not bite or crush food; they merely tear it into smaller pieces with the bill, often swallowing the pieces along with the bones, feathers, and fur. The wide pharynx and greatly expandable gullet enable the bird to swallow quite large pieces which are passed to the crop where some digestive processes occur before passing on to the stomach. The stomach consists of an antechamber (proventriculus), where the food is broken down by the chemical action of various digestive secretions, and the gizzard (ventriculus) where it is ground up mechanically. In view of the type of food consumed by raptors, the gizzard does not have such strong muscular walls as in gallinaceous birds or typical seed eaters. From the stomach, the food passes to the small intestine and then the large intestine, which is somewhat enlarged at the end, forming the chamber called the cloaca, into which also open the urinary and reproductive tracts. Urine is collected in paired kidneys and discharged through two ureters into the cloaca. There surplus water is reabsorbed and it is transformed into a whitish material which is passed out of the body together with the faeces. The excrement of raptors is very loose and is ejected from the anal opening to considerable distances. Raptors, like other birds, have no urinary bladder.

Undigested particles such as fur, the chitinous remains of insects, feathers, claws, beaks, and bones are regurgitated from the stomach in the form of pellets. Some raptors (vultures), however, are capable of digesting even quite large bones.

The food eaten by birds of prey varies widely as do the methods of procuring it. Raptors generally feed on other animals, mostly birds and mammals. Some hunt their prey by pursuing and attacking other birds in the air. Such a potential airborne victim usually has time to see the approaching danger and to conceal itself. This manner of procuring food is typical of falcons. Other raptors, such as the Goshawk, and Sparrowhawk, employ the element of surprise. Flying low, close above the ground, they pounce on prey in the branches of trees or on the ground. The diet of smaller raptors is even more varied. Besides small birds and mammals, they also capture flying insects or collect insects on the ground. One such example is the Hobby.

There are many food specialists that eat not only the most widely varied types of animals but even food that is quite unusual for birds of this group. Some raptors hunt fish (Osprey, Sea Eagle), others are content with frogs (harriers). The Short-toed Eagle and the Secretary Bird are fond of snakes and lizards. Some raptors take young birds as well as eggs from nests, as do crows. The large Asian eagle *Ictinaetus malayensis* has feet and claws so shaped that rarely does an egg slip from its grasp when it is robbing a nest. The Harpy Eagle of South America, and certain other raptors such as the Monkey-eating Eagle, are particularly fond of monkeys and sloths. Found throughout South and Central America are buzzards of the genus *Buteogallus* which prey on crayfish, crabs, frogs, and fishes in the shallow waters of the sea coast and rivers. Places where they eat them are

Fig. 4 Details of the head of (A) a Goshawk and (B) a Peregrine Falcon. The Goshawk hunts its food in the treetops or close above the ground so that its eyes are turned forward and are topped by prominent bony arches.

The eyes of the Peregrine Falcon, which hunts its prey in the air, are placed at the sides of the head and protrude rather like periscopes, giving a wide field of vision.

often covered with small piles of the cracked animals' shells and claws. The Honey Buzzard, too, has an interesting way of obtaining food. With its strong claws, it tears apart the nests of wasps and bees to get at the insects and larvae inside. It supplements this diet with a vegetation sidedish of fruit. The Palmnut Vulture, *Gypohierax*, of Africa feeds mostly on the fruit of the oil palms. The fare of the Everglade or Snail Kite, *Rostrhamus sociabilis*, of Central and South America would not be scorned by a French epicure. With its long, down-curved upper mandible, it extracts from their shells the snails that form the major part of its diet. Even nocturnal animals are not safe from diurnal raptors. In the Malay peninsula and in Africa there are birds of the genus *Machaerhamphus*, that in the evening as well as at night capture flying bats. When attacking, they fly under their prey, turn over feet uppermost, and sink their claws into the bat's body from below.

The last group of food specialists is the Old World vultures and New World vultures including the condors.

These birds do not hunt live prey, nor are they properly equipped for that purpose, but consume the carcasses of animals and birds.

The physical strength of raptors enables them to capture enough food for themselves and their offspring as well. Some, however, have adopted methods of procuring food that may be termed parasitism. Vultures may be considered parasites in some measure in that they often feed on the remains of a carcass killed and left by some large beast of prey. A more pronounced example of such parasitism may be found among the kites which, though they can also hunt live prey, prefer to take prey caught by other raptors. The Common Buzzard also sometimes obtains its food in this way.

The wings of raptors

The types of food a bird eats and the method of procuring it are reflected in the body structure. In raptors this is reflected particularly in the shape and arrangement of the feet, wings, and other parts of the body. The top surface of a bird's wing is convex and the underside concave. It is thicker near the leading edge than the trailing edge. This shape is called an aerofoil. As the bird moves forward, the flow of air over this surface produces lift.

In comparison with aircraft, a bird's wing has many other features that improve the flow of air over the wing and also the power of flight. These include the bastard wing, the slit-like arrangement of the wing tips, and the ability to change the shape of the wings and the body by manipulating individual feathers.

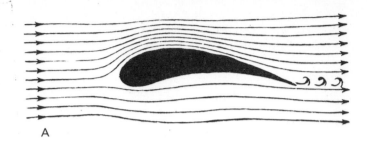

A

Fig 5   Diagram of the forces acting on the wing in flight. Air flowing over
the upper (convex) surface of the wing flows faster than that over the lower
(concave) surface exerting lift as shown in B.

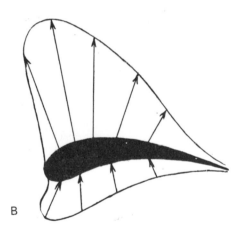

B

Raptors that hunt flying objects, mostly birds, must be
capable of great speed. Narrow, crescent-shaped, pointed
wings, possessed by falcons, for example, are best for fast,
dashing flight. Quite different are the wings of the Goshawk
and Sparrowhawk, which capture their prey among trees.

27

Here, the long, narrow wing would be of little use and that is why the wings of the Goshawk are short, fairly broad, and rounded with quills spread apart at the tips. From an aerodynamic viewpoint, their construction is not ideal because their shape permits neither rapid, active flight nor soaring and gliding. It is, however, excellent for manoeuvering, for sudden, rapid turns, immediate take-off, and sharp braking in the smallest free space. Such wings give the bird great speed for short distances, but are not suited for continuous pursuit. The Goshawk's and Sparrowhawk's ability to manoeuvre is improved by the long, wide-spreading tail which serves as an excellent rudder.

In the third group of raptors, the wings are more or less adapted for soaring. Typical birds of this group — eagles and vultures — have long, wide wings that cannot be used for sudden turns or rapid acceleration but are perfect for support in soaring flight high in the sky where they remain aloft on the lookout for food. Vultures descend to a carcass in slow, gliding flight whereas eagles press the wings to the body and swoop down upon their prey.

All raptors use both the two main forms of flight that are characteristic of most birds (only hummingbirds employ a rapid whirring motion reminiscent of the flight of some insects which enables them to hover in one spot as well as to move from one place to another). The first form of flight is

Fig. 6 The flight of raptors:
soaring flight when on the lookout for food (1 White-tailed Eagle. 2 Common Buzzard, 3 Peregrine Falcon);
plummeting dive when attacking prey (4 Golden Eagle, 5 Osprey, 6 Hobby, 7 Peregrine Falcon);
hovering flight when on the lookout for food (8 Osprey, 9 harrier, 10 Kestrel).

effected by beating the wings at regular intervals. During this movement the wingtips describe an ellipse. At the downward stroke, the bird propels itself forward and the lift begins to take effect. This form of flight is used mainly by raptors that capture their prey in the air (falcons) or by sudden attack among trees (Sparrowhawk). That does not mean that they would not also soar and glide. Under favourable conditions, some are quite good at this form of flight, too. The Sparrowhawk flies by beating its wings, alternating this with gliding and soaring. The flight of buzzards and harriers is similar.

Hovering, which is characteristic of certain falcons (Kestrel) as well as buzzards, kites, and the Osprey, is a modified form of flapping flight. It is also used by hummingbirds, shrikes, terns, larks, flycatchers, and gulls. Basically, it is flight in a single spot. The bird points its tail towards the ground and begins to flap its wings rapidly forward and back. The bird's movement is controlled also by steering with its outspread tail and the bird remains suspended in the same spot. It usually takes advantage of the headwind as well. This type of flight is used mainly in seeking prey on the ground or in water.

Soaring or gliding flight is more specialized. Here the bird remains high in the air for hours, taking advantage of the slightest breeze and of all the thermals — rising columns of warm air caused by the uneven heating of the land or sea by the sun. Such a soaring bird, however, is to a certain degree dependent on the whims of nature. If conditions are not favourable for soaring and gliding then the bird does not apply this form of flight. In deserts, for example, an interesting phenomenon may sometimes be observed. When the sun begins to heat the stones and sand in the morning, soaring raptors take to the air in a definite order.

30

First to fly up are the kites which, because of their small weight, are borne aloft quite easily by even slight thermals. As the air becomes hotter and the thermals become stronger, the smaller and lighter vultures take to the air, and finally the largest vultures, which need very strong thermal currents to become airborne. American vultures, eagles, buzzards, and other raptors with long, broad wings are also excellent gliders.

Pilots of sports gliders sometimes come across soaring raptors and together they seek the best thermal updrafts that make soaring easier and faster. They then rise in an ascending spiral one behind the other. To the pilot's annoyance, it often happens that a soaring buzzard or vulture begins to increase the speed of its climb without any sign of physical exertion and is soon circling high above the aircraft. Try as he might the pilot is unable to catch up. This faster climb under the same weather conditions is explained by the improvement of the bird's aerodynamic qualities when it seems able to improve the airflow around the wings and body, attaining the necessary power without any visible movement. On the other hand, the bird can worsen its aerodynamic qualities for the purpose of sudden braking, a rapid dive to the ground, and the like.

Aircraft designers are well aware of the salient features of birds and are always trying to improve the efficiency of aeroplanes. From his very first attempts at flight man copied the structure of the bird's wing and still does today, though in a different form. American aircraft designers decided they would follow an airborne bird of prey in a glider and would measure and record the basic data of its flight. They installed the necessary recording instruments, a film camera, and a transmitter in the aircraft and the pilot took it up among soaring vultures. The bird chosen for the purpose was the American Black Vulture, *Coragyps atratus*, which is not exactly the best of soarers. During the flight the pilot observed and filmed changes in the shape of the wings in the various stages of flight and at the same time reported the recorded values via the transmitter. At the conclusion of the experiment, when the recorded data had been computed and evaluated, the designers were astonished. The vulture's body and wings, which appear to be clumsy and of poor design behaved in the air like a thin plate. The resistance of the vulture's body to the air was practically nil. When the vulture's wing was placed in an air tunnel, normally used for observing the airflow around the wings of a newly designed aeroplane, however, the results were so poor that no aircraft could take off from the ground if it had wings of the same design. This finding confirms the superiority of the living creature which can mould the shape of the body surface according to the resistance of the surrounding air and create ideal conditions for flight.

If we wish to evaluate the flight characteristics of raptors objectively we cannot speak in terms of good or poor fliers because we would then be intentionally disregarding the fact that the method of flight is determined by the biological needs of each species. The various forms of flight are the result of adaptation to a given way of life in a given environment, the chief role being played by the type of food the bird eats. That is why we should find it hard to find poor fliers among the raptors. All are capable of covering vast distances, and in spring, during the courting period, they sometimes circle high in the air for hours on end performing various spectacular feats.

The social behaviour of raptors

Raptors live in a wide variety of habitats. They live, hunt, and nest in woodlands, in open, park-like areas, in bush-covered plains, in rocky mountains, in reed beds in lakes and rivers, on the rock islands of the open seas, as well as in arid deserts. Some are slowly becoming adapted to changing conditions and may even be found in the immediate vicinity of man — in towns and villages.

Most birds of prey live a solitary life, forming pairs only during the breeding period. Old World and New World vultures as well as certain other raptors such as the Lesser Kestrel, *Falco naumanni*, are, to some extent, gregarious. Old World and New world vultures form loose associations when they are circling on the lookout for food. More marked association in larger groups may be observed when food is found and the birds converge at a given spot, or when some individuals have discovered the benefits of living in the neighbourhood of man and gather in groups close to places such as refuse dumps, sewage works, and slaughterhouses. Some raptors form more firmly estab-lished associations and nest together in small colonies (vultures, kites). Loose flocks, formed mostly in the autumn by those raptors that migrate regularly to distant wintering grounds or by those that move to more favourable hunting grounds, may also be considered social units.

A typical social unit is the one formed at the start of the breeding period. At this time, usually in the spring, birds pair to raise a brood. Raptors seem to be monogamous, that is, each bird has only one mate. Once the union is sealed the pair remains together for many years, that is, unless one or the other of the partners dies. This tie is particularly strong in the case of large raptors and, as a rule, the pair returns to the same nesting site for many years.

The prenuptial period is a time of courtship displays which are generally performed in the air but sometimes also on the ground. The male, and often also the female, execute various acrobatic feats in the air — steep dives, rapid climbs to great heights, seemingly helpless, plummeting falls, soaring in stiff poses, simulated attacks, hovering flight in one spot, releasing and catching of twigs, upside-down flight, and so on. In fact, the performance consists of the transmission and receipt of signals to which each of the engaged parties must respond suitably at the proper moment. This exchange of information lowers the barriers between the two partners as they prepare for copulation.

The raptor's nest

When birds have found a mate they begin building a nest. Those which have already raised broods before may use one of their old nests. Young birds nesting for the first time must build a new one unless they take over an old crow's nest. Raptors build their nests in various places. Some nest in trees (Goshawk, Sparrowhawk, buzzards), others also in tree hollows (Kestrel); eagles and vultures often nest on rock ledges in mountains; in the tundra and steppe, some raptors nest on the ground (northern falcons, the Tawny Eagle); harriers seek the shelter of reed thickets in the middle of swamps. Last but not least, raptors are also known to nest on buildings which offer suitable shelter. Occasionally, we may come across the nest of a Kestrel, or sometimes also a falcon, on the tower of an old castle, the belfry of a church, or in some other such place.

Building a nest is no easy task, especially in the case of large birds of prey, and once constructed it is often used for several years in succession. As the birds add to it every year, the nest may become very large indeed. Sometimes a nest is occupied every year by only one species of raptor; at other times, it may be used by several different birds of prey. Thus, for instance, one year a nest may be used by the Osprey, the following year by the Sea Eagle, and eventually by a kite. Many raptors are not particularly keen on building nests of their own, however, and use the abandoned nests of other birds. The Peregrine Falcon, for example, never builds a nest in trees, but takes over an old nest of a magpie, crow, heron, raven, or other birds.

The shape and size of the nest, as well as the material used for its construction, depend upon the size of the raptor. The nest is usually built by both partners and the framework is made of twigs gathered on the ground or broken off from trees as the bird flies past (eagles). Inside this framework, there are layers of finer material, and the innermost lining, on which the eggs and later the nestlings lie, is a soft cushion of dry grass, moss, animal fur, feathers, bits of cloth, paper, and other industrial wastes. Kites use broken reed stems to build their nest. There is a shallow depression in the centre of the nest and the edge is raised and is repaired constantly throughout the nesting period.

The offspring and their parents are not the only occupants of the nest. Apart from the many different insects that feed on the decaying food remains inside the nest, there may also be true subtenants because the spaces between the branches of large raptors' nests are ideal nesting sites for sparrows, starlings, wagtails, and even the Great Tit. The small South American parrot, the Green Parakeet (*Myiopsitta monachus*), even builds whole colonies in the lower parts of a raptor's nest, raising its brood there without the slightest fear. This phenomenon is known as social parasitism. The best example of social parasitism of raptors is the relationship between the South American Black-headed Duck, *Heteronetta atricapilla*, and the Chimango Caracara, *Milvago chimango*. The duck places its eggs in the nests of other ducks, herons, coots, rails, and ibises as well as in the nest of the aforesaid raptor, which is located on the ground. The duck's egg is much larger than that of its host, and is differently coloured, but still it is accepted by the latter as its own. It is extremely resistant to cold. On hatching the young duckling must abandon the nest, after which it usually joins the young of other ducks. If it abandons the nest when the raptors are away, all is well. Nor will anything happen to it while it moves about inside the nest, even when the adult bird is present, because the contents of the nest are taboo for the raptor. As soon as the duckling climbs over the edge of the nest, however, crossing the boundary of the 'protected area', it is pounced upon and killed by the raptor. This often happens when the female begins feeding the duck, offering it a choice bit of meat. The duckling, however, is not accustomed to being fed and is so frightened by the adult bird's behaviour that it dashes to the edge of the nest. In an instant, it is killed and is fed to the raptor's own offspring.

It is hard to believe that birds preyed upon by raptors could nest in their immediate vicinity. And yet we find further such examples; for instance, falcons, buzzards, kites, and even eagles have been known to nest in colonies of herons, cormorants, or crows, and there are even instances when a raptor and its prey — a falcon and heron — have been found nesting in the same tree. Rarely, however, does a raptor seek its food or rob nests within the colony.

Nesting

As a rule, raptors raise only one brood a year. The number of eggs they lay is largely influenced by their mode of life, the type of prey they feed on, and above all by the abundance of prey. Large raptors generally lay one or two eggs, whereas some smaller species may lay six or seven eggs. The geographical location also plays a certain role. In northern regions where conditions are more rugged and there is less hope of survival, a raptor will lay more eggs than the same bird in the southern part of its range. In the case of raptors that feed on small rodents the size of the clutch is influenced by the availability of food. When rodents are plentiful, birds of prey lay more eggs than in lean years when they may not lay any eggs at all.

The partners take turns incubating the eggs, though the female carries the greater part of the load. As a rule, the male sits on the eggs only for a brief period in the morning, at noon, and in the evening. The male Honey Buzzard relieves his mate at regular intervals. The male harrier and Sparrowhawk, on the other hand, incubate only on rare occasions but diligently keep the hen and later the newly hatched nestlings supplied with food.

The female usually begins incubating when the first egg is laid. Eggs are laid at intervals of forty-eight to seventy-two hours so that, in the case of a large clutch, the young hatch in succession, often at intervals of several days. The last to hatch are usually pushed aside by their elder and stronger siblings at feeding time and, as they rarely succeed in feeding, their development is retarded and in the end they either die of exhaustion or else are attacked, killed, and finally eaten by the other occupants of the nest. Cannibalism is quite common among raptors and is one of the factors that regulate the numbers of a given species. It is generally closely linked with the abundance, or rather lack of food. Apart from man, raptors have few natural enemies, so that their numbers would be regulated by food supplies. In some cases, man is proving to be such a grave danger to birds of prey that some species are on the verge of extinction. Man has brought this about either directly, by hunting and shooting, or indirectly, through the use of various chemicals in agriculture. Raptors are very sensitive to certain pesticides and as a result lay fewer eggs or eggs that are unfertilized or have a very thin shell that is easily cracked.

The incubation period for raptors is fairly long. In the case of smaller raptors, it is about four weeks, whereas for larger raptors, such as vultures, it is fifty to fifty-five days. This is somewhat risky from the viewpoint of the preservation of the species but raptors have few natural enemies and the adult birds are able to protect the nest without much trouble. For example, the Hooded Crow, which weighs twice as much as the Sparrowhawk, incubates for only seventeen or eighteen days, whereas the female Sparrowhawk sits on her eggs for thirty-one to thirty-three days.

Care of the young

Raptors are nidicolous birds, that is, the young remain in the nest for some time after hatching and have to be fed and cared for by the parents until they are fully grown. The young of nidifugous species are capable of independent activity from birth; they leave the nest and feed themselves almost immediately with the parents merely guiding and watching over them. Young raptors are hatched with a cover of soft down and are able to see from the moment of birth. The first days they are very sensitive to cold and are kept warm by the hen. During this period, the male procures food for the entire family by himself, passing it to the female which tears it into small pieces before feeding it to the young. She holds the food in front of the nestlings and they take it from her bill. Later the hen joins her mate in hunting for food and gives it to her offspring whole so that they will learn to pluck it clean and tear the flesh. In some species, the parents share the duties of attending the young. Both forage for food and bring it to the nest but the female prepares it and passes it to the nestlings. If she dies while they are still so small that they are unable to tear up the kill then they die of hunger because the male, even though he brings them enough food, is unable to prepare it for them. Vultures, which often have to carry food great distances, fill their expandable crop and then disgorge it into the beaks of their offspring. Carrying it in the crop enables them to bring far more food than they can carry in the beak; their feet are not adapted for carrying food at all.

The period it takes for raptors to raise their offspring is usually long. Smaller raptors, such as the Kestrel and Sparrowhawk, attend the young for about a month; in larger species, such as vultures and the Secretary Bird, it may be as long as four months. When their wing quills grow, the young birds begin to practise flight movements and shortly after abandon the nest. It is at this time that they weigh the most. They soon begin to lose weight, however, because adult birds feed them far less often to force them to search for food by themselves. At the same time, they become much better at flying and the instinct to attack moving creatures begins to assert itself. As soon as the young are fully independent, the parents stop feeding them. Smaller species attain full maturity in their first year. In larger species, the young do not begin to nest until their fourth or fifth year.

Man and raptors

Raptors are of great importance to man. Many of them feed on rodents and regulate the numbers of these creatures that man views as pests. The great strength of raptors and their hunting ability have also been made use of by man. He caught large birds of prey, trained them, and used them to hunt birds and mammals. In the past he used them to procure food, and in some places does so to this day. Falconry, hunting with trained falcons, however, is again becoming popular in some countries, not as a means of procuring food but as a sport. Many species of raptors are already on the verge of extinction and the present worldwide trend to protect these birds is to be encouraged. Many European countries have already provided for the strict protection of raptors and their shooting is forbidden. In the remaining European countries everything indicates that the total protection of raptors will become law there too.

OWLS

Owls and man

The similarities in mode of life, in particular diet and hunting methods, between owls and diurnal raptors have led people to believe that the two groups are closely related. In reality, however, this is not so. Their closest allies are the rollers and nightjars. Owls are referred to as nocturnal birds of prey or even nocturnal raptors because, like the diurnal raptors, they have strong, grasping feet with sharp, curved talons, a similarly down-curved beak, and their diet consists mainly of warm-blooded vertebrates.

To man the owls' most undesirable characteristic is that they hunt and eat mammals and birds of all sizes. Therefore, they have met with the same fate as birds of prey and are still shot and killed despite the fact that they are of great benefit to man in that they destroy small rodents. Owls' unpopularity may also be due to the fact that they generally hunt at night or at dusk, though some species of owls seek their food even during the day. Man regards with distrust all creatures that are active at night, that have better eyesight, and are better adapted in any way than he is, because even in familiar surroundings he does not move about as surely at night as during the day. Not only do owls see well in very poor light, they also have very acute hearing and a good sense of smell, which often provide them with more exact and detailed information than does their eyesight. Their noiseless flight (the result of the sound-deadening filaments at the tips of the flight and contour feathers) as well as unpleasant calls and cries are more reasons why owls have been regarded with suspicion and were associated with witchcraft in tales and legends. In ancient times, they were regarded as symbols of wisdom, probably because of the large head, conspicuous eyes, and the appearance of looking wise.

The largest and smallest owls

Owls as a group, which does not comprise very many species, differ from raptors in a great many ways. They never attain the size of the largest birds of prey. The smallest owls are smaller than a sparrow. The Least Pygmy Owl, *Glaucidium minutissimum*, is only 12 centimetres long. Medium-large owls, about the size of a crow, Jackdaw or pigeon, weigh 200 to 700 grams and have a wingspread of 90 to 110 centimetres, in other words, about the same as that of the Peregrine Falcon. Included in this group are the Barn Owl, Tawny Owl, and Long-eared Owl. The largest owls (Eagle Owl, Snowy Owl) weigh 2.5 to 3.5 kilograms and their wingspan of 150 to 180 centimetres is the same as that of the Spotted Eagle, Short-toed Eagle, and Osprey. The Fish Owl of northern China and northern Japan has a wingspan of as much as 2 metres.

Owls' flight

There are no differences in the plumage of the male and female owl but female owls are always larger and heavier than males. Their coloration is identical and even juveniles are coloured the same. Even though raptors are not brightly coloured, their plumage is more striking than that of owls, which consists of an unobtrusive mixture of greyish, brownish, rusty, or whitish hues that give the bird its protective, 'bark-like' coloration. Perching motionless in a tree, an owl often looks like the broken, lichen-covered stump of a dry branch (Long-eared Owl, Scops Owl). Only the Snowy Owl has a more striking coloration, in as much as that term can be applied to its practically all-white plumage. Here, too, the coloration is adapted to the bird's environment.

There are two reasons for this cryptic colouring. Firstly, a bright and striking combination of colours serves no purpose for the owls' nocturnal way of life, and in the daytime, when the birds usually rest, it could even prove harmful. Small birds will mob all owls. Moreover, many owls are preyed on by certain raptors and bright plumage would only increase their vulnerability.

An owl's plumage has one remarkable feature which is closely connected with the type of food the bird lives on. If you were to pluck an owl clean you would discover that its body is quite small, the impression of size being created by the long, silky, thick feathers. This plumage, however, does not serve only as insulation against cold. Owls living in the tropics have just as dense plumage as those of the arctic regions. In flight, however, the wing quills of diurnal raptors and songbirds produce a whistling sound that often is too high-pitched to be detected by the human ear. Fieldmice, mice, ground squirrels, and other rodents preyed on by owls have very good hearing, however, and are able to perceive ultrasound. Therefore, the owl's flight must be very silent. The bird can be seen and it can be heard when it claps the wings together as it attacks, but in normal flight the wings make no sound at all. This is because of the bird's soft flight feathers which are covered with a thick layer of fluffy down. Thus, the wing quills and tail feathers of an owl can always be distinguished from those of other birds. It is not yet clear, however, if the flight is also silenced by the comb-like fringe on the forward edge of the first two wing quills.

The eyesight of owls

The owl's nocturnal mode of life has led to the maximum development of its sight and hearing. These are the two senses owls use in hunting prey, though it is hard to say which predominates. Both are equally well developed and probably each supplements the other according to the given situation.

Of all the vertebrates, birds have the most highly developed eyes. The eyeball is only rarely spherical. In fact, the owl's eye is usually described as the tubular type. The whole eyeball is covered with a tough, white, fibrous membrane called the sclera, except for the transparent cornea at the front. Beneath the sclera is the middle coat of the eye called the choroid, a dark, vascular membrane ending in front in the ciliary body with a muscle that contracts the pupil. The innermost coat of the eye and the part most important for seeing is the retina with its light-sensitive cells. Situated inside the eye behind the iris is the lens, and the space between this and the retina is filled by a transparent, jelly-like substance called the vitreous humour.

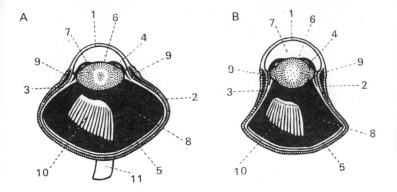

Fig. 7 Diagram of the eye of birds of prey:
(A) a raptor's eye; (B) an owl's eye.
A conspicuous feature of the owl's eye is the cylindrical shape of the eyeball.
1 cornea 2 sclera 3 choroid coat 4 iris 5 retina 6 lens 7 aqueous humour 8 vitreous humour 9 bony ring in the sclera 10 pecten.

The owl's most conspicuous feature is its large head and eyes. The space containing the brain, however, is very small. The head has to be large enough to accommodate the huge eyes which give it its remarkable eyesight. A large eye can make the most of any available light in poor light conditions. The owl's eye has a large lens and rapid-functioning iris which opens up in the dark and closes in bright daylight, regulating the amount of light passing through the pupil. In owls, the pupil of each eye can be contracted separately.

A large, spherical eyeball would take up too much space so that the size of the lens and cornea is increased by the tubular arrangement of the eye. The remarkably large cornea and lens and comparatively small retina increase the eye's light perception capacity. The larger the lens and the cornea, the more light rays that enter the pupil, and the greater the light perception capacity of the eye. It is incorrect to say that owls cannot see during the day. On the contrary, the owl's sight in daylight is just as good as a human's and often even better.

A measure of light perception capacity of the eye can be determined by dividing the surface area of the retina by that of the cornea. The smaller the ratio between the two the greater the light perception capacity. In man the eye's light perception capacity is expressed by the number 13.5, the Kestrel's is 11.5, a pigeon's 10.0, the Tawny Owl's 4.0, and the Barn Owl's 3.5.

The more nerve cells there are in the retina the keener the vision and the greater the resolving power of the eye. The number of nerve cells in the retina serves as an indication of the visual acuity of the animal. The retina of a salamander has about 2500 cells per square millimetre, that of a frog 95 000, a man's and a cat's has 400 000, and that of the Tawny Owl 680 000 per square millimetre. The nerve cells of the retina are of two kinds, called rods and cones. Rod cells control the acuity of vision but register images only in black and white. Cone cells are sensitive to colour. Diurnal creatures have a far greater number of cones whereas nocturnal animals have practically none.

In reptiles and birds there is a comb-like tissue (pecten) around the transparent, jelly-like part of the eye at the point of the optic nerve where there are no light-sensitive cells. It is thought that this provides nourishment to the eye and, by shading part of the retina, enables the eye to follow a flying object better and more quickly even against such a pale and uniform background as the sky.

The acuity of vision is determined also by the action of the lens and cornea. Bulging of the cornea and movement or change in the shape of the lens cause the eye to focus so that the optical image on the retina is as clear as possible. In birds, the eye is focused by flattening or thickening of the lens.

Specific data about the sensitivity of the eyes of vertebrates to light are scant. Experiments with the Barn Owl, however, have shown that they can see their prey even when it is very dark. The Barn Owl can see and catch a mouse when the intensity of light is only 0.000002 lux (the lux is a unit of illumination). Many diurnal birds are unable to see well even when the intensity of light is 46 000 times greater. This means that the owl's eye is capable of utilizing even the slightest bit of light though to the human eye it may seem like impenetrable darkness. Not even owls, however, can see in total darkness.

The owl's telescopic eyes have all the prerequisites for seeing at night. The cylindrical eyeball, however, is much less mobile in the socket than a spherical eyeball. Hence, the owl's eyes face forward and have a narrow field of vision. Whereas a Kestrel, with eyes at the sides of its head, has an angle of view of 220 degrees and is able to take in a wide range at a single glance, the Barn Owl's field of vision embraces an angle of only 160 degrees. In owls, however, this is made up for by their stereoscopic vision and the ability to turn their heads in a wide circle. The special arrangement of the first two vertebrae enables them to twist the head around a full 270 degrees, so that an owl can be sitting with its back turned towards a person and yet be facing him.

Birds with eyes at the sides of the head have a wider field of vision but they see objects only in two dimensions. Perfect orientation and the judging of distances require stereosco-pic vision. Man, too, has stereoscopic vision because his eyes also face forward.

Most birds can take in practically the whole panorama, almost 360 degrees, but their binocular vision is fairly limited. In parrots it embraces an angle of 6 to 10 degrees, in other birds 10 to 25 degrees. Raptors, and above all owls, which are able to see a sector of 70 to 80 degrees, are an exception.

Also of interest is the way owls close their eyes, which generally have a bright yellow or yellow-orange iris, though sometimes it may be a dark hue. Whereas other birds close their eyes with their lower lid, owls 'blink' with their light-coloured upper lid. They also possess a third eyelid, the nictitating membrane, which slides from the inner to the outer corner of the eye.

Owls are long-sighted and their ability to see close objects is poor. That is why they feel their prey with the tactile bristles that grow profusely at the base of the bill and at the gape. That is also why the young do not exhibit any reaction to proffered food until it touches the tactile bristles.

The hearing of owls

Owls' second important sense is hearing. Unlike other birds, owls have markedly developed ear lobes — flaps of skin covered with special, stiff feathers. The ear lobes serve not only to cover the ear opening but can also be moved to improve hearing. They are often asymmetrically positioned on the head, especially in owls, that locate their prey

Fig. 8 Head of the Eagle Owl showing the ear lobe.

primarily by sound, thus aiding the exact location of the noise. Besides the ear lobes, hearing is also improved by the characteristic facial disc made up of concentric circles of feathers round the eyes which function like parabolic reflectors in gathering and concentrating sound waves. This sound trap increases the owls' sound-catching ability about fifty times compared with that of a duck. The owl's ear is adapted mainly to detect the high-pitched squeals emitted by the small rodents on which owls feed and is not tuned to hear other owl noises, which are low pitched, to the same extent. On the other hand, the Eagle Owl, which hunts larger animals, and the Fish Owl, which preys on fishes, are not well adapted to hear the high-pitched notes of mice.

The perfection of the owl's hearing may be illustrated by a written record of the observation of a blind Tawny Owl. This sightless bird reacted to the seemingly noiseless clenching of the fingers; in other words, it heard the rubbing of the moving tendons and muscles. It also reacted to the sound made by the movement of the lungs in the chest cavity.

Man is able to locate the direction from which a sound is coming. Nocturnal hunters, such as owls, also use this means to find moving prey. The owl's directional hearing, however, is far more accurate than a human's. Of all living birds, owls have the best directional hearing. An owl needs to be able to pinpoint the position of a prey animal quickly in the dark. It is able to determine the location of a sound to an accuracy of 1 degree. An owl perching 20 metres from a gnawing fieldmouse can locate its position to within a segment of 35 centimetres. At a distance of 10 metres it can pounce with great accuracy because the victim's position will have narrowed down to a segment of 17 centimetres. This may seem unbelievable but that is only because of the imperfection of the human ear. Man can determine the location of a sound in only two dimensions, in the horizontal plane. If the sound comes from above he must turn his head to locate it. The owl has no such difficulty because it perceives sound in three dimensions.

Sound coming from some point other than directly from the front or from the rear reaches the ear furthest from the sound slightly after reaching the nearer ear. At the speed of sound of 330 metres per second at sea-level, this represents only a fraction of a second, yet the owl's brain registers this delay, processes it, and uses the information to direct its line of attack. Directional hearing in owls, then, is based on the perception of the time difference between the instant the sound of 330 metres per second at sea-level, this represents other, and in the case of nearby sounds by the difference in the loudness of the sound on the two sides. In man, this is a brief moment lasting about 0.00003 seconds; owls, however, perceive differences of even shorter duration.

Owls hunt their prey either from an elevated perch or by slow flight just above the ground. They grasp it with their

Fig. 9 Foot of the Long-eared Owl. The fourth (outer) toe is reversible. Prey is grasped with two toes in front and two behind. The toes are feathered down to the talons.

talons but not crosswise like raptors. Their grip can be likened to that of the Osprèy, the victim being held lengthwise with two toes in front and two at the back. The owl's outer toe is reversible allowing a more secure hold on a moving object.

The owl's digestion

Unlike raptors, owls have no crop in which to store food so that they keep the food they are unable to consume by the nest or in handy cavities. The owl's diet usually consists of small mammals, but owls also eat birds, insects, amphibians, and, in rare instances, fishes, crabs, or carrion.

Owls do not usually tear the flesh of the small animals they feed on, but swallow them whole after first crushing the body slightly with the beak. Only large owls, which sometimes catch a hare or duck, must first tear the kill into smaller pieces. Owls always swallow the flesh of their victims together with the fur, feathers, scales, and hard elytra. An owl's stomach does not secrete enough hydrochloric acid to dissolve these hard substances, however, and the indigestible parts are regurgitated in the form of pellets — pressed solid lumps of fur, feathers, bones, claws, chitin, and scales. The owl's digestive system is so adapted to this method of feeding that if the bird were to be given a diet of pure meat it would become ill and might even die.

Owls usually regurgitate two pellets daily, one at night at the spot where the owl digests its food, the other at the spot where it hides during the day. Owls always regurgitate such a pellet before setting out to forage for food. Digestion is so rapid that indigestible remnants are regurgitated within three hours of eating. Large piles of these pellets may often be found on the ground under an owl's perches. The shape and colour of the pellets serve to determine not only the species of owl but also the food it eats. The bones of vertebrates are clean and white and easily identified. From an analysis of owl pellets, zoologists even succeeded in identifying small mammals which were not known to exist in a certain area or even to exist at all.

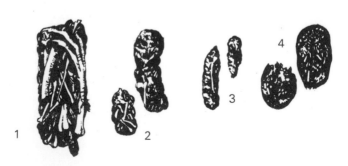

Fig. 10 The pellets regurgitated by owls contain the undigested parts of the animals they eat (fur, feathers, bones, claws, the chitinous remains of insects) 1 Eagle Owl 2 Tawny Owl 3 Little Owl 4 Barn Owl.

Nesting behaviour of owls

The Short-eared Owl is the only European owl that builds a nest; other owls lay their eggs in the abandoned nests of other birds, in tree hollows, rock crevices, attics, or ground cavities. Owls usually have one brood a year. The eggs are always pure white and spherical. Tropical species lay only two or three eggs, whereas central European owls lay three to five eggs, and owls of the arctic regions may lay ten, or as many as thirteen in times of plenty. Most European owls begin nesting in March or April, some as early as February, and the breeding season usually ends in May or June. If there is abundant food, owls may have two broods a year, and in meagre years the clutch is smaller or the birds may not breed at all.

As a rule, the female incubates and cares for the young alone. She begins incubating as soon as the first egg is laid; thus, the young show great differences in size because the eggs do not hatch at the same time. The period of incubation varies from twenty-five to thirty-five days depending on the species. The young are hatched with eyes shut and covered with a thick coat of down. They abandon the nest before they are able to fly but remain in its vicinity, letting their parents know where they are by uttering special cries. Owls have ringing voices that are not particularly pleasant to the human ear. Some hoot, others make gobbling, wailing, barking, or crying sounds. Only very few have a pleasing musical trilling. Other forms of vocal expression are clacking of the bill and slapping of the wings when courting.

Owls are mostly solitary birds, although the Short-eared and Long-eared Owls do sometimes congregate in groups. There are 134 species of owls divided among thirty genera in all parts of the world. Most are to be found in woodlands but some inhabit the barren plains, snow-covered tundras, inaccessible cliffs, and even human habitations. They occur in both lowland and high mountain regions.

Owls' importance to man

The author does not support the theory that the existence of an animal species should be determined or defended by its benefit or detriment to man. All that is found in nature has its place, be it pleasant or unpleasant to man. The importance of owls, however, is so great that it deserves to be stressed with renewed emphasis. Their diet makes them efficient agents in controlling rodent populations, aiding man as only few other animals do.

RAPTORS

Egyptian Vulture

Aegypiidae

Neophron percnopterus

Birds do not generally use tools to carry out the tasks essential to their lives. There are exceptions to every rule, however, so that among birds there are specialists that do make use of some kind of tool. The Woodpecker Finch, *Camarhynchus pallidus*, of the Galápagos Islands uses a cactus thorn to impale and pull out insects hidden under the bark of trees. The Black-breasted Buzzard Kite, *Hamirostra melanosternon*, of Australia is fond of eggs. When it comes upon an incubating Emu, it chases the hen off with feigned attacks, then grasps a strong stick or stone in its talons, flies up and drops the stick on to the nest time after time until it hits and shatters the eggs.

The Egyptian Vulture behaves in a similar way. With its beak it takes eggs from the nests of pelicans or flamingos, knocking them against a hard object until the shell cracks. If it comes across an Ostrich egg which is too big to grasp in the beak it takes up a rock and hammers at the shell until it cracks. In the case of an unincubated egg it carefully drinks the contents, and if it contains an embryo then it swallows this 'delicacy' whole, Eggs, however, are not its main food. Generally, it feeds upon the carcasses of dead animals as do other vultures. Because it has a fairly weak bill, however, it has to be content with smaller and softer pieces of flesh. In Africa, it may often be seen around towns and villages where it feeds on refuse, serving a useful purpose where sanitation conditions are poor.

Egyptian Vulture

continued

The Egyptian Vulture is distributed throughout practically the whole of Africa, the Middle East, and India and Turkestan. In Europe it breeds in Portugal, Spain, southern France, Italy, Sardinia and Corsica, the Balkans, and Rumania. Only occasionally does it visit central Europe. Birds from the northern regions are migrant, mostly those from Europe and North Africa which winter in equatorial Africa. The autumn migration takes place in August and September and they return to the nesting grounds usually in March.

In flight the Egyptian Vulture is easily distinguished from other European vultures by the dirty white plumage with black wing tips. Immature birds are brownish. Like most vultures, it has a bare face and throat. It measures 58 to 66 centimetres in length, weighs about 2 kilograms, and has a wingspan of 145 to 160 centimetres.

It usually breeds on inaccessible cliffs, building its crude nest from mid-March to April. The clutch usually consists of only two rufous-brown, marbled eggs which both birds take turns incubating. The young hatch after forty-two days and are fed in the nest for about three months.

Griffon Vulture

Aegypiidae

Gyps fulvus

On warm mornings, when many animals and birds are already abroad foraging for food, Griffon Vultures are usually still under the rocky overhangs where they roost. Their time to hunt has not yet come because the thermal updrafts are not strong enough for them to fly. The ground must be warmed for some time before they are able to lift their 7 or 8 kilograms aloft on their 2 to 2.5 metre wingspread with scarcely a wing beat.

A soaring vulture keeps an eye on the ground below for any sign of a dying animal and it also watches the movement of other carnivorous creatures, because flying ravens, kites, or running hyenas can lead it to food. In addition it also observes the other vultures in the area. As soon as one of them spots a carcass (from a height of 1000 metres the Griffon Vulture can distinguish an object the size of an apple, and from a height of 3650 metres an animal the size of a rabbit), it glides down to the ground. Its descent alerts the other vultures in the air and they follow suit. As if linked by invisible strings they converge, sometimes as many as several dozen of them, around the carcass.

Its great strength enables the Griffon Vulture to make a hole in the belly of a dead cow or antelope quite easily. Then it puts its head inside and begins pulling out the entrails. As the number of its companions increases, however, it plunges its head into the carcass and feasts without any delay. It gorges itself and has to rest afterwards. Then it flies off to water where it drinks its fill and bathes.

Griffon Vulture

continued

This sight may be seen in south and north-west Africa, the Near East, and central Asia, where the Griffon Vulture is most plentiful. This bird, measuring 97 to 104 centimetres in length, is to be found also in Europe where it breeds in small numbers in the Iberian Peninsula, in Sicily, and Sardinia, in the Balkan Peninsula, in Rumania, and in southern Hungary.

The male and female have similar, brown-coloured plumage and long neck covered with short, whitish down. The ruff around the neck is white in adult birds and brown in immatures. Between January and March, the Griffon Vulture lays its single egg on an inaccessible cliff ledge. The young bird hatches after forty-eight to fifty-four days and remains in the nest for 125 to 130 days during which time it is cared for by the parents.

European Black Vulture

Aegypiidae

Aegypius monachus

The irregular supply of food has had a marked influence on the vultures' adaptability. They are able to go without food for days or to be satisfied with only quite small animals. When they come upon a carcass they literally gorge themselves, however, consuming such a quantity of meat that they must then rest for some time and if they must fly up for any reason, they have to regurgitate some of the food to lighten the load before they are able to take off. This is true of the European Black Vulture, a giant weighing 7 to 12 kilograms, with a wingspan of nearly 3 metres. When vultures converge upon a carcass, it becomes a scene of indescribable furor with the birds emitting harsh cries and flapping their wings as they fight among themselves over a scrap of meat. On one occasion twenty-nine vultures picked the carcass of a Fallow Deer clean within seventeen minutes.

The European Black Vulture has about the same range as the Griffon Vulture except that it is absent from southern Africa. In Europe its distribution is limited to the Iberian Peninsula, the Balkans, Crimea, and certain islands in the Mediterranean. The plumage is a uniform brown, as is also the ruff, from which emerges the bare, bluish neck ending in a fairly small head.

Unlike the Griffon, the Black Vulture nests in trees so that there is no competition for nesting sites. In February or March the female lays a single egg, weighing about 25 grams, which she incubates for fifty to fifty-five days. The young bird does not leave the nest until it is four months old. It requires a great deal of parental care. During the first few days after hatching, one or the other of the parents is always on the nest keeping the nestling warm with its body or else shielding it from the burning rays of the sun with half-spread wings.

European Black Vulture

continued

The young bird is usually supplied with plenty of food. It is disgorged by the adult birds into the nest, torn into smaller pieces, and then offered to the nestling. The European Black Vulture swallows meat together with smaller bits of bone and gives the same to its young. Sometimes, however, the piece of bone is so large that the bird refuses to swallow it. The partially digested food is taken by the nestling directly from the beak. Water is also an important part of the young bird's diet which it gets from its parents by pecking at the leathery corners of their beaks. This triggers a slight nauseous reaction in the adult birds causing a thin stream of water to flow from the corners of the beak which the young bird catches and swallows with rapid movements of its bill.

When it is about two months old, the young bird begins to react to unfamiliar approaches and to adopt the typical defensive pose. At the age of four months it begins to practise flight movements either in the nest or on a nearby branch. After its first flight, however, it continues to return to the nest for some time, where it feeds, rests, and spends the night.

Lammergeier

Aegypiidae

Gypaetus barbatus

The steep slopes of high mountain peaks are so dangerous that now and then even such sure-footed creatures as the Ibex and Chamois lose their footing and fall to their death, the remains of their bones being mute witness of the tragic happening. The more careful observer, however, will note that sometimes such a pile contains a greater number of bones of different sizes and shapes, such as a cow's rib, a horse's vertebra, the skull of an Ibex, and many remains of various animals. He will know that he has chanced upon a rare find, that is, the place where the Lammergeier shatters the large bones of dead animals into smaller pieces so that they can be swallowed more easily.

It is generally known of vultures that they feed on carrion and can pick a horse's carcass clean to the bone. If the Lammergeier is the first to discover such a carcass, however, then it naturally starts eating the soft, fleshy parts. Before long it is joined by other vultures and although it is one of the largest birds of the group it gives ground to its more agressive companions and waits for the leftovers. Usually, all that remains is the bare skeleton. For the Lammergeier, however, this is still quite edible. Its stomach secretes such a quantity of acids that bones are completely digested. If a bone happens to be too big to swallow whole the Lammergeier grasps it in its talons, flies up, and drops it from a height to shatter on the rocks below. It is in such places that you can find the mixture of animal remains because not all the large bones shatter when they fall. The shells of turtles are shattered in the same way.

Lammergeier

continued

The Lammergeier is one of the largest of the Old World vultures, weighs 5 to 7 kilograms, and makes its home in the European Alps, Spain, the Balkans and the mountains of Africa, the Middle East, and central Asia. It measures 102 to 104 centimetres and has a wingspan of more than 2.5 metres. The adult bird is blackish-brown above, the wings and tail are almost black, and the underside is rufous yellow. The head is creamy yellow with a black band across the eyes and a black beard. In flight, the Lammergeier is easily distinguished from other vultures and eagles by the long, wedge-shaped tail and narrow, pointed wings held slightly bent.

The nest is usually placed in an inaccessible spot in a rock cavity or under a rocky overhang. The Lammergeier does not start breeding until its fifth year. In December to February it lays one or two eggs. The young hatch after fifty-five to fifty-eight days and remain in the nest until the age of 110 days.

White-tailed or Sea Eagle

Accipitridae

Haliaeetus albicilla

The eagle's build, strength, and bearing are so imposing that it has often been called king of the air or king of birds and has been included in the coats-of-arms of princes, kings, and nations.

One of the largest birds of prey and the largest of the eagles is the White-tailed or Sea Eagle, weighing 4 to 6 kilograms. The smaller and lighter male measures about 70 centimetres in length, the larger and heavier female more than 90 centimetres. The wingspan of a soaring bird may be as much as 250 centimetres. The long, broad, straight wings terminate in seven primaries spread apart like fingers (emarginated) and pointing slightly upwards in flight. Adult birds have earthy brown plumage, yellowish head and neck, and pure white, bluntly wedge-shaped tail. The immature bird is dark to black-brown with a brown, white-spotted tail. The tail gradually becomes whiter with age and by the fourth to fifth year, when the young birds attain maturity, it is pure white.

In flight, the wing beats are slow and sluggish, but the White-tailed Eagle is an expert at soaring. Its flight, however, only seems to be slow and heavy because even a crow cannot keep up with the eagle carrying prey, and the crow's speed is about 60 kilometres an hour. The eagle does not capture its prey in the air but by flying close above the ground or water and attacking it in a sharp dive. As its name implies, the Sea Eagle feeds on fish. This is also testified to by the tarsus which, unlike in the eagles of the genus *Aquila*, is not feathered down to the toes. It does not dive into the water as often as the Osprey and usually catches its prey near the surface. There are few freshwater fishes that it cannot overpower; it has even been known to capture pike weighing 12 to 15 kilograms. With such a weight, however, it cannot fly up into

White-tailed or Sea Eagle

continued

the air and usually swims with the aid of its wings to the shore, where it then proceeds to tear the flesh from the victim. A 5 to 6 kilogram fish, however, poses no such problem and the eagle has no trouble becoming airborne. It also hunts mammals and birds, particularly when the waters freeze over. It will not scorn a fieldmouse or Blackbird, and can just as well handle a heron, swan, stork, fox, otter, small dog, or wild piglet. It consumes about 700 grams of meat daily, including carrion.

It is found mainly near expanses of water, large inland lakes, and on the seacoast. In Europe it sometimes occurs in the northern coastal areas of East and West Germany, its range extending eastward throughout the whole Palaearctic region. It is a bird of the lowlands and is usually not found more than 300 metres above sea-level.

Eagles are monogamous birds. The nest, used several years in succession, is 3 to 5 metres high, up to 2 metres across, and weighs as much as 600 kilograms. In February or March, the female lays one to three whitish eggs which she and her partner take turns incubating for thirty-four to forty-two days. The young birds remain in the nest for eighty to ninety days.

Pallas' Sea Eagle

Haliaeetus leucoryphus

Accipitridae

The vast area from the Ukraine across practically the whole of central Asia is the home of Pallas' Sea Eagle, a relative of the White-tailed Eagle, which occurs as a vagrant in the western parts of the USSR and very occasionally also in central Europe, Poland, and in the north in Finland and Norway. It measures about 75 centimetres in length, weighs 2 to 3.5 kilograms and has a wingspan of about 2 metres. It, too, is all brown, with pale head and neck, but the tail is longer than the White-tailed Eagle's and slightly rounded, not wedge-shaped. It is brownish black with a broad, white band (10 to 12 centimetres wide) in the middle.

Both sea eagles have the same way of life. Pallas' Sea Eagle hunts the same animals and also builds its nest in trees, though sometimes it nests in reeds. It is not a typical inhabitant of the lowlands, however, and in some places is found in uplands. In Tibet, it nests at elevations of up to 5000 metres. In such areas, it cannot hunt fish and soars over the slopes on the lookout for dead animals.

Birds from the southern parts of its range of distribution begin to breed in October, November, and December. Palaearctic populations do not start building nests until the end of February or March. The nest is only slightly smaller than that of the White-tailed Eagle and the edge is almost always adorned with green twigs during the time it is occupied by the young. The two to three eggs are incubated for thirty to thirty-two days and it takes seventy days before the young are fully independent.

Golden Eagle

Aquila chrysaetos

Accipitridae

The growing world population and growing demand for food have had a marked effect on the methods of farming. Chemical agents are being used with increasing frequency and though this improves crop yields it also has its disadvantages. Man ingests toxic substances either directly (in his food) or indirectly (via herbivores that feed on plants sprayed with toxic pesticides) and these can gravely endanger his health. The same applies to large animals, including birds of prey. In Scotland, for example, ornithologists discovered that pesticides have a disastrous effect on the reproduction of the Golden Eagle. Pesticides used for dusting plants were eaten by animals that the eagles fed on and the concentration of poisons in the birds' bodies increased daily. This caused thin-shelled eggs which were so fragile that they were crushed by the slightest pressure. During the period pesticides were used only 29 per cent of the observed eagles successfully hatched their eggs. The eggs of 36 per cent of the birds were broken and 41 per cent did not breed at all. When the use of these pesticides was prohibited, the reproduction rate returned almost to normal: 70 to 80 per cent of the eagles raised their broods successfully. It was also determined that the concentration of poisons in the eggs was 66 per cent lower following the prohibition of their uses.

The Golden Eagle is called the king of birds not only because of its size, weight, and majestic bearing but also for its superb mastery of the air. Taking advantage of thermal updrafts, it climbs rapidly and without sign of effort above the high mountain peaks and then without a single wing beat soars across several valleys, sometimes covering a distance of 13 kilometres. Its flight is far faster than it seems. The impression of slowness is caused by the

Golden Eagle

continued

vast spread of the wings, which may be as much as 2 metres. It was determined that in gliding flight the eagle attains a speed of 150 kilometres per hour and if there is a favourable wind from behind as much as 190 kilometres per hour. When diving to the attack the speed of an eagle weighing 3.5 to 4.5 kilograms was estimated as being up to 320 kilometres per hour.

The Golden Eagle is found in North America, Asia, and in a narrow belt in north Africa. In Europe it used to nest at lower elevations but gradually retreated to more remote areas and today breeds in the Alps, Carpathians, Scandinavia, the mountains of Scotland, and the Iberian and the Balkan peninsulas.

The adult bird is brown with a golden-yellow head. Immatures are a paler hue and have a light spot on the underside of the wings and a broad, dark band at the tip of the white tail. It builds its nest on cliffs. In late March or April the female lays one or two, very occasionally three eggs, which both parents take turns incubating for forty-three or forty-four days. The young remain in the nest up to eighty days, being incapable of flight before that.

Imperial Eagle

Aquila heliaca

Accipitridae

Steppes with deciduous woodland groves such as are found in the southern parts of European Russia, south-eastern Europe, Asia Minor, and eastward as far as north-western India and Mongolia, are the native habitat of the Imperial Eagle. It also nests in the Iberian Peninsula, the Balkans, and Morocco, and it is also found in central Europe where it breeds in smaller numbers in the eastern parts of Czechoslovakia and northern Hungary. Here too, however, the character of the countryside is undergoing marked changes and the Imperial Eagle is often disturbed and persecuted by man, which has caused it to leave its hunting grounds, that are rich in steppe rodents, and to hide its nests in the more densely wooded hills. Luckily it is not restricted to a diet of ground squirrels like the Steppe Eagle and finds enough food even at higher elevations. Its diet includes mammals ranging in size from a mouse to a young hare, marmot, or fox. During the breeding period, it often brings its offspring various birds. It will even eat frogs, insects, and occasionally carrion. It consumes 400 to 600 grams of food daily, sometimes being content with only a Turtle Dove, at other times consuming as much as 1200 grams of meat at once.

The method of hunting depends on its surroundings and on the type of prey. The Imperial Eagle either perches motionless on a haystack or low tree on the lookout for prey or it circles in the air and attacks the victim in a headlong dive. Sometimes it hunts frogs and insects on the ground in the manner of the Lesser Spotted Eagle; in the case of larger animals, it hunts them in low flight like the Golden Eagle or the White-tailed Eagle. When making a surprise attack it is even capable of catching a partridge in the air.

Imperial Eagle

continued

The Imperial Eagle ranks among the largest of the group and is only slightly smaller than the Golden Eagle. It has a wingspan of 180 to 210 centimetres, measures about 80 centimetres in length, and weighs between 2.5 and 4 kilograms. The plumage is brownish black, the nape and hind neck are straw coloured (in older birds almost white). There is a white patch on the shoulders (the western forms from Spain and north Africa also have a white patch at the bend of the wings). The whole underside of the body is dark and there are six to seven grey stripes on the dark tail which is terminated by a broader dark band. Young birds are buff coloured with darker streaks; there is no white in their plumage.

The carelessly built nest, measuring 80 to 130 centimetres across, is usually placed high up in trees. The two, sometimes three eggs are whitish with violet, brown, and reddish blotches. The young hatch after six weeks and fledge after a further eight to eleven weeks.

Steppe Eagle

Accipitridae

Aquila rapax nipalensis

It is interesting to note that the life cycle of the Steppe Eagle is closely linked with the seasonal cycle of the Pouched Marmot. Spring, when the animals emerge from their burrows, marks the arrival of the brown Steppe Eagle from its winter quarters in southern Asia. Throughout the summer and well into autumn it feeds almost exclusively on these rodents, only very occasionally catching something else. In the steppe regions of eastern Europe, central Asia, China, and India, Pouched Marmots are so plentiful that the bird can afford to confine itself to such a limited diet.

The Steppe Eagle is rarely seen in central Europe and it is by no means easy to identify. Though it is larger than the Spotted Eagle, with a wingspan of about 180 centimetres and weight of 2.5 to 4 kilograms, only a keen observer is able to distinguish the birds in flight.

The nest is built on the ground on a rise that affords a good view of the countryside. It is a flimsy structure and the two, very occasionally three, eggs, coloured grey-violet and reddish brown, often lie directly on the ground encircled by a ring of loosely woven branches. The young hatch after about forty-five days and abandon the nest at the age of sixty days. Only thanks to the surplus of food during the breeding season are most of the young birds reared with success.

Spotted Eagle

Accipitridae

Aquila clanga

Many species of birds resemble one another so closely that even a trained observer has difficulty distinguishing them at first glance. One such example is the Spotted Eagle which is very similar to the Lesser Spotted Eagle in size and coloration. The Spotted Eagle is browner than the Lesser Spotted, which has lighter plumage chiefly on the crown and underside, but this is of little help in identifying it in the field. The Spotted Eagle is rather heavier in build and measures 66 to 74 centimetres in length with a wingspan of 160 to 180 centimetres. Immature birds have a greater number of larger, whitish spots than juvenile Lesser Spotted Eagles.

The Spotted Eagle is a native of eastern Europe and the southern part of Siberia as far as the Far East. It is a migratory bird and journeys to Egypt, Asia Minor, and southern Asia for the winter. Paired birds remain together for life. The nest may be as much as 110 centimetres high and equally wide and is placed in tall trees. Sometimes the Spotted Eagle makes use of another raptor's nest. In May the female lays two eggs with duller markings than those of the Lesser Spotted Eagle. The young hatch after about six weeks and, unlike the Lesser Spotted Eagle's, both leave the nest after sixty-three to sixty-five days. The diets of the Spotted and Lesser Spotted Eagle are very similar.

Lesser Spotted Eagle

Accipitridae

Aquila pomarina

Europe is the home of five eagles of the genus *Aquila* which are typical representatives of this group of raptors. One is the Lesser Spotted Eagle weighing 1.5 kilograms, measuring 63 centimetres in length and with a wingspan of 150 to 165 centimetres. Eagles are often falsely accused of being extremely aggressive birds of prey constantly killing weaker animals. An eagle's imposing appearance with its powerful build, strong talons, and characteristically down-curved bill may have given rise to this idea. The prominent supra-orbital ridges augment this impression. There is little truth in the old belief that the eagle has an insatiable desire to kill. In fact, it takes a good deal of effort for eagles to obtain enough food for themselves and their young. Often they have to do without and their young die of hunger. The diet of the Lesser Spotted Eagle consists of small rodents, fieldmice, mice, ground squirrels, and hamsters.

The Lesser Spotted Eagle nests in tall trees in central Europe from eastern Germany, Bohemia, and Austria to the middle of European Russia, the Balkans, Asia Minor, the Caucasus and northern Iran. Another form breeds in India. European birds spend the winter in the African savannahs round the equator.

Their return to the nesting grounds is announced by a series of piercing cries and pairs may be seen soaring in huge, spiralling circles in their typical flight silhouettes with broad, stiffly outspread wings.

Lesser Spotted Eagle

continued

In late April or early May the female usually lays two eggs, the first always larger and heavier than the second and with more distinct markings, coloured brownish violet. She begins incubating as soon as the first is laid and, because the second is laid after an interval of three to four days, there is about the same period between hatchings. Incubation takes thirty-eight to forty-one days and the duties are mostly performed by the hen. As a rule, both eggs are hatched but about eight weeks later only the stronger firstborn leaves the nest. There are two opinions as to why the younger offspring does not survive. One is that the elder sibling instinctively climbs on top of the weaker bird and conceals it, thereby preventing proper nourishment of the youngster, which grows continually weaker until it dies, being perhaps fed then to the elder bird by the hen. The other opinion is that about two weeks before fledging the young birds have a heightened aggressiveness that asserts itself against all moving objects within a range of about 50 centimetres. The younger eagle tries to evade the attacks of its sibling until its movements bring it to the edge of the nest from which it then tumbles to its death.

Bonelli's Eagle

Hieraaetus fasciatus

Accipitridae

Man has domesticated a variety of animals for many purposes. Some have served as beasts of burden and as a source of food and clothing, others guard and protect his property and are used in hunting. Man has even used certain birds of prey for this sport. In central Asia, hunters train and use Bonelli's Eagle to hunt gazelles The bird spots a gazelle easily even from a distance of a kilometre, overtakes it, and plummets headlong after it in a steep dive. It brakes just in time to sink its talons in the gazelle's head, halting it in its tracks, and within minutes it is killed by the pack of dogs.

Bonelli's Eagle is rarely found in central Europe. It nests in southern Europe, Africa, and Asia, preferring open, park-like country where it places the nest (up to 2.5 metres in diameter) on cliffs, though sometimes also in trees. In February to March the female usually lays two pale, rust-spotted eggs which she incubates for about forty days. The young leave the nest at the age of two months.

Bonelli's Eagle is about the same size as the Spotted Eagle (its wingspan is about 170 centimetres) but has differently coloured plumage. The dark brown back contrasts sharply with the grey tail terminated by a black band. The whitish underside is marked with dark, longitudinal streaks and resembles the plumage of a young Goshawk. Immatures are brown above and rusty brown below.

Booted Eagle

Accipitridae

Hieraaetus pennatus

The Booted Eagle is a small bird that could easily be mistaken for the Rough-legged Buzzard in the wild. A closer glance, however, would reveal that the eagle's tail is straight, not rounded like the buzzard's, and unbarred. The Booted Eagle occurs in two colour phases. In both, the upper side is brownish grey with pale-tipped feathers and white scapulars. The dark phase has brownish-black underparts with paler tail. The light phase has creamy yellow, slightly streaked underparts, light wing linings, and dark primaries. The bird's wingspan is 110 to 120 centimetres, the length 46 to 53 centimetres, and the weight about 700 grams in the case of the male and almost 1000 grams in the case of the female.

The Booted Eagle nests in south-western Europe, the Balkans, and from south-eastern Europe as far as central Asia. It is also found in India and Africa. A very rare visitor to central Europe, it nests in small numbers in Hungary and eastern Czechoslovakia.

It hunts small mammals, birds, lizards, and insects in hilly areas and more lowland, rolling country. The nest is generally placed in trees, sometimes also on cliffs. The two, very occasionally three, whitish eggs are incubated for about thirty-five to thirty-eight days and the young are cared for by the parents until the age of fifty-four to sixty days, by which time they are able to fly.

Short-toed Eagle

Circaetus gallicus

The silhouette of the Short-toed Eagle resembles that of a Buzzard or Honey Buzzard but this eagle is such a rare bird in some areas that you might not think to identify it by its coloration and flight. If you were to see it flying with a partly swallowed snake hanging from its bill on its way to feed its young, you would have no doubts about its identity.

In flight the Short-toed Eagle is a large, pale-coloured bird. Its wingspan of 150 to 170 centimetres is practically the same as that of the Spotted Eagle. The medium-long tail spreads slightly at the tip and has three conspicuous dark stripes on the underside. The head is exceptionally large and the disc of facial feathers gives it an owl-like look. The top parts are greyish brown with black primaries. The belly and underside of the wings are almost white with black tips to the underside of the primaries. The white belly is in sharp contrast to the dark breast and this is also evident in flight. The Short-toed Eagle is more robust than a buzzard, measuring about 70 centimetres in length and weighing about 2 kilograms, that is, twice as much as a buzzard. In appearance, it is a sort of intermediate between the eagles and the buzzards.

The huge wings and large wingspan indicate that the Short-toed Eagle is an excellent flier. Its powered flight is not very fast and is slightly reminiscent of the light, reeling flight of owls. It is an expert at soaring, however. Sometimes, it may be seen hovering in a single spot, being one of the few raptors able to do so without any perceptible movement of the wings. If there is a horizontal current of air flowing head on, the bird adjusts the angle of its wings so that the resultant lift is equal to the weight of its body and maintains its stability by only slight movements of the primaries and the tail.

Short-toed Eagle

continued

These feats are part of its method of hunting. Hovering in one spot helps it to survey the terrain and locate prey, which in the case of the Short-toed Eagle consists of various kinds of reptiles. As soon as the bird spots, say, an Adder, it flies to the ground, graps it with its short, clawed toes, and crushes or bites off the creature's head with its bill. It even hunts very poisonous snakes but is not immune to the effects of the poison.

The Short-toed Eagle is a migratory bird that breeds in Europe (except Britain and northern areas), its range extending eastward as far as south-west Siberia, central Asia, and northern India. It also nests in Africa. European birds return from their winter quarters in central Africa in April. The nest is placed in trees and the clutch consists of one egg. It is incubated for a period of about forty-five days and the young bird fledges after ten to eleven weeks.

Common Buzzard

Accipitridae

Buteo buteo

Man's false ideas about raptors are gradually being corrected but in many countries they are still firmly established. The Buzzard does catch a partridge or pheasant on occasion and can cause great damage, but this happens only in winter during severe frosts when the earth is covered with a thick layer of snow, and partridges are weak and hungry. Being unable to get at its usual fare — fieldmice and mice — because of the snow cover, the Buzzard attacks the partridges. It has no other choice because it does not fly fast enough to catch swifter, small birds. In milder winters when there is no snow cover, the Buzzard takes practically no notice of partridges because it can hunt fieldmice. Data on the analysis of food eaten by the Buzzard show that 96 per cent of its diet consists of harmful rodents, and the remainder of fowl, wild game, and other vertebrates.

The Buzzard is the commonest raptor in Europe apart from the Kestrel. It is found throughout the whole of Europe, its range extending in a broad belt across central Asia to the Far East. It also breeds in Asia Minor, the Himalayas, and certain west African islands. It is a bird of the woodlands even though when foraging for food it is generally seen in open country. Tall, old beeches, oaks, pines, and other forest giants are where the Buzzard places its nest, often using it several years in succession, in which case the nest is always repaired and added to so that it may be as much as 70 to 80 centimetres high and about 1 metre in diameter.

Common Buzzard

continued

The Common Buzzard is a moderately large bird with broad wings measuring 51 to 56 centimetres in length. The male weighs 600 to 1000 grams, the larger female 700 to 1200 grams. The wingspan is 120 to 140 centimetres. The plumage coloration is variable. The back is usually dark brown, the underside pale with dark spots. The spots may vary in number and the birds may be almost black to almost pure white. The dark brown tail is barred and has a broad, dark terminal band.

Buzzards are generally resident, although Scandinavian and Russian breeders migrate and individual birds may be vagrants or migrants. February is the month when they return to their nesting grounds, immediately commencing their courtship display which includes a variety of aerial acrobatics and is accompanied by a drawn-out mewing call. In April to May the female lays two to three rough-shelled eggs spotted with grey, ochre, and violet, which she incubates for about thirty-three days. Only now and then is she relieved by the male. The young leave the nest at the age of six to seven weeks but remain with their parents for some time after.

Steppe Buzzard

Accipitridae

Buteo buteo vulpinus

In addition to public exhibitions, ornithological collections in central European museums contain large numbers of buzzard skins lightly filled with sawdust, with wings drawn close to the body and legs outstretched to make it easier to store these comparative skins. The specimens include a wide range of variously coloured buzzards such as the Steppe Buzzard. The Steppe Buzzard is a geographical race of the Common Buzzard distributed from northern Scandinavia across Finland, European Russia, and western Siberia to the upper Yenisei River, and the Altai. In central Europe, it may be seen only in the autumn on its way to its winter quarters in southern Asia and eastern Africa and in spring on the return trip to its nesting grounds. Migrating birds, however, usually pass unnoticed because of their resemblance to the Common Buzzard, and proof of their occasional presence in the area is only obtained in the museum laboratory.

This buzzard shows as much colour variation as the Common Buzzard, ranging from light-coloured individuals to ones so greatly spotted as to be almost a single dark hue. Rust is the predominant colour, being especially pronounced on the upper tail surface. In flight, the wings appear narrower and more pointed than those of the Common Buzzard and the wing beats are faster. The habits of the two forms, however, are very similar.

Rough-legged Buzzard

Accipitridae

Buteo lagopus

The northern parts of the Old and New World, mainly the tundras from Scandinavia to Kamchatka and from Alaska to Newfoundland, are the home of the larger, sturdier Rough-legged Buzzard. The male weighs an average of 900 grams, the female about 1200 grams, and the wingspan is 130 to 155 centimetres. The legs are thickly feathered down to the toes giving the bird its name. The colour of its plumage differs markedly from that of the Common Buzzard, though it, too, varies somewhat. The general coloration is much lighter than the Common Buzzard's and the lining of the wings is white with distinct black carpal patches. The head is also a pale colour. Also distinctive is the tail which is white with a broad black terminal band. Another reliable diagnostic feature is the large dark shield on the belly.

The Rough-legged Buzzard does not breed in central Europe, appearing there only in winter from October to March. Its breeding habits, similar to the Common Buzzard's, are greatly influenced by the food conditions. Only its choice of nesting site differs markedly — about 80 per cent of all Rough-legged Buzzards nest on the ground or on cliffs, the remainder in trees.

In years when the lemmings of the northern tundras are plentiful then the Rough-legged Buzzard, which eats lemmings almost exclusively, has enough food, and only few of these birds may be seen in Europe. In such years it also lays a greater number of eggs, raises more young, and the population expands. Lemmings, however, show cyclic population variations so that the buzzard's period of feasting is usually followed by a time of hunger. Lack of food in its home territory compels the buzzard to seek out more southerly regions. Often, whole flocks make their way south and if there are no fieldmice to be found or if a thick

Rough-legged Buzzard

continued

layer of snow covers the ground even in central Europe, then the hungry birds attack wild game.

Diminution of the food supply is reflected in the breeding of the Rough-legged Buzzard. If the lemming population falls to very low levels the buzzards will not pair at all and may not even appear on their nesting grounds. When the lemming population is small the birds form pairs, arrive at the nesting grounds, and often even build a nest, but do not breed. When the lemming population is below average buzzards have clutches of two to four eggs but usually abandon the nests. In peak years when the countryside is swarming with lemmings, the size of the clutch is larger (three to six eggs) and the number of birds that are reared with success is two to four per nest. In quite exceptional years the buzzards may lay as many as four to seven eggs and raise four to five young.

Long-legged Buzzard

Accipitridae

Buteo rufinus

The territory north of the Common Buzzard's range is inhabited by the Rough-legged Buzzard and the area to the south by the Long-legged Buzzard. Differences between them are very slight so that the Long-legged is difficult to distinguish from the Common Buzzard.

The Long-legged Buzzard measures 61 to 66 centimetres in length, weighs 1100 to 1500 grams and has a wingspan of about 150 centimetres. With its long, broad wings, it resembles in flight a small eagle rather than a buzzard. At a distance, it appears to be a light-coloured bird, particularly the light phase, but even darker individuals have a distinct white band on the underside of the wings. Unlike the Common Buzzard, the tail is a single colour — rufous, greyish, sometimes almost white. In young birds the tail is barred. In its native habitat — the dry, open plains and steppes of eastern Europe, Greece, Asia Minor, central Asia and North Africa — it occurs in three typical colour phases. The brown and rufous phases may occur in shades of varying intensity whereas the dark to almost black phase exhibits no such transitions.

The Long-legged Buzzard is rarely seen in central Europe, where it appears only as an occasional vagrant. It spends the winter in the warmer regions of eastern Africa and southern Asia. The nest is placed on the ground, on cliffs, and in trees. The three to four eggs are laid in March to April. Further details of the bird's nesting habits are as yet unknown.

Honey Buzzard

Accipitridae

Pernis apivorus

Walking through the woods, you may sometimes chance upon a hole in the ground filled with the remains of a honeycomb, or come upon wasps flying back and forth around their demolished nest. The culprit may have been a badger or a fox, or perhaps it was the Honey Buzzard — another food specialist among raptors, feeding mainly on wasps and their larvae. The peculiar diet and method by which the Honey Buzzard procures its food is reflected in certain of the bird's physical features.

The Honey Buzzard is about 50 to 57 centimetres long, weighs 400 to 1050 grams, and has a wingspan of 125 to 140 centimetres. It shows such great variation in coloration that practically no two individuals are the same. The upper parts are nearly always brown, the underside, however, ranges from near white to brownish red. The rounded head lacks the typical raptor's expression. The shape of the head is evident even in flight, another feature distinguishing it from the Common Buzzard being the more outstretched neck .The greyish-brown or brown tail is barred with bands of varying width; there are one or two bands near the rump and a broad dark terminal band. There is also a dark band on the trailing edge of the wing. The bars on the tail of the Common Buzzard, with which the Honey Buzzard is often confused, are regularly spaced.

The Honey Buzzard's method of procuring food is unique among raptors. It flies low over the ground on the lookout for wasps emerging from their nests. When it spots a nest, it alights close by, and quickly but carefully approaches it. After examining the hole in the ground, it sets about enlarging it by scraping the soil away with its feet, sometimes using its beak as well. It completely ignores the attacks of the angry wasps, catching them skilfully

Honey Buzzard

continued

with its feet, sometimes using its beak as well. It completely
ignores the attacks of the angry wasps, catching them skilfully
with its beak and swallowing them whole or biting off their tail
ends. It is protected against stings by its thick plumage and by the
facial feathers which, unlike the soft feathers found in other birds
of prey, are stiff and strong and arranged like scales. The Honey
Buzzard's foot resembles the foot of fowls, the strong toes being
equipped with massive but short, flat claws. The non-feathered
part of the leg is covered with strong, horny scales which no sting
can penetrate. Besides wasps the Honey Buzzard also eats other
insects, small vertebrates, and often even fruit.

The Honey Buzzard is a migratory bird inhabiting the forests of
practically the whole of Europe. It is absent only in the
southernmost parts of Spain and Italy and in northern Scandinavia. It returns from its winter quarters in tropical Africa
fairly late, usually not until May, whereupon it begins to
build its nest in the tops of trees. A broad construction
up to 1 metre across, the nest generally contains two eggs
with brownish red marbling, which are incubated by both
partners for thirty to thirty-five days. The young birds abandon
the nest at the age of five to seven weeks. September and October
are the months when the Honey Buzzard departs for its winter
quarters.

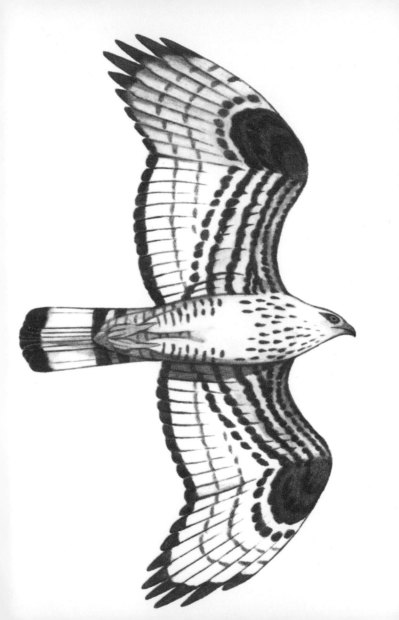

Goshawk

Accipiter gentilis

Accipitridae

The Goshawk hunts everything it is able to cope with. It will not scorn a small mouse or Chaffinch and will also venture to attack even a hare, hen, Capercaillie, or heron. Mammals make up 10 per cent of its diet, birds the remainder. The Goshawk is not popular with hunters because they view it as a competitor and often kill it even when this is prohibited. Thankfully, the Goshawk is not easily caught. Even though it is not exactly rare in Europe's forests, it leads such a secretive life that it is hardly ever seen. Only occasionally does it venture into open spaces and then it crosses them quickly. It does not perch in elevated spots as does the Buzzard. Its hunting grounds are dense woods.

The Goshawk looks like a large, heavy, short-tailed Sparrow-hawk. The male has a darker upper side than the female and lacks the reddish colouring of the Sparrowhawk on the underside. The sexes differ in size. The much larger female weighs 1 to 1.2 kilograms and has a wingspan of about 120 centimetres whereas the male weighs a mere 0.75 kilogram and has a wingspan of about 1 metre. It is sometimes suggested that this difference in size makes it possible for the Goshawk to make the most of the available food supply in the hunting grounds which cover an area of 12 to 19 square kilometres. The female hunts larger prey whereas the smaller and more agile male is skilled at surprising and catching smaller animals in the dense undergrowth.

In flight the Goshawk bears a slight resemblance to the Buzzard, mainly in the size of the female. Viewed from below, it appears to be pale in colour whereas in the Buzzard the dark spots stand out against the light background. The Buzzard likes to soar in large circles on the lookout for fieldmice in the fields. The Goshawk, on the other hand, usually flies a straight course close

Goshawk

continued

above the treetops and tries to take its victims by surprise. Its short, rounded wings and long tail, which can be fanned out wide, allow it to manoeuvre skilfully among the trees and branches.

The Goshawk is found in wooded areas in Europe, northern and central Asia, and North America and also breeds in north Africa, occurring in many geographical forms throughout its vast range.

The nest is a well-concealed structure placed high up in tall trees deep inside the forest and is used for a number of years. The birds add material to the nest every year so that often it is as much as 1 metre high and the same in diameter. The male's courtship performance consists of magnificent aerial acrobatics accompanied by a loud cry. In April the female lays three to four dirty grey to greenish-white eggs which she usually begins to incubate when the second is laid. The young birds hatch after thirty-five to thirty-eight days and are fed by the female; the male merely plucks the prey clean and passes it to his mate at a specific place. By the time they are forty days old the young birds are already quite adept at flight. They differ from the adults in that they have a brown back and ochre underside covered with brown streaks.

Sparrowhawk

Accipiter nisus

Accipitridae

A grey-blue streak suddenly flashes in the treetops on the village outskirts and then regular wing beats carry the bird high up into the air in the direction of the nearby forest. It is the Sparrowhawk visiting one of its regular hunting grounds with a host of agitated Swallows, martins, wagtails, and sparrows in its wake. Uttering loud cries they fly above, behind, and alongside the Sparrowhawk but none ventures to attack and none flies down below, for they all know by instinct that to come close means certain death. A sudden thrust of the hawk's leg to the side and the victim is caught fast in its long, sharp-clawed toes. The Sparrowhawk continues unconcerned in its flight, however, and its pursuers fall back as soon as they see that their homes are no longer in imminent danger.

The instant the Sparrowhawk attacks in a fast dive sparrows flee into the undergrowth though they are not safe even there, but they find the courage to pursue it far out into the fields. This is because the Sparrowhawk hunts and catches its prey by sudden attack and is capable of great speeds only for a short distance. In open country small birds have time to make their escape. Even the Sparrowhawk is apparently aware of its inability of rapid pursuit for a greater length of time and it usually pays no heed to the pestering birds flying in its wake.

The Sparrowhawk is a comparatively common European raptor found in all types of woodland, though it prefers coniferous forests which afford better concealment for its nest. It breeds in all of Europe, north Africa, and a large part of Siberia. Some birds are resident, others are vagrants or partial migrants.

Sparrowhawk

continued

The smaller male, which resembles a Cuckoo in size and coloration, weighs an average of 140 grams and has a wingspan of 60 centimetres. The larger female weighs 240 grams on average and has a wingspan of up to 75 centimetres. She is dark grey above and light coloured on the underside with dark barring. Her mate is similarly coloured but is rufous below and has reddish pantaloons.

The Sparrowhawk returns to its nesting grounds in March, the time of courting when the birds perform their various antics to the sound of sharp, penetrating cries. The nest is usually located close to the forest edge or a clearing between 5 and 20 metres above the ground. In May and June it contains a clutch of four to six eggs with brown, grey, and violet marbling. The young hatch after thirty-three days and are fed a variety of small vertebrates by the female, which first tears the flesh into small pieces. They leave the nest after twenty-four to thirty days and are fully independent at the age of six weeks.

Levant Sparrowhawk

Accipitridae

Accipiter brevipes

Most people do not identify raptors according to their characteristic features but lump them together under general headings. If the raptor is a bird the size of a Turtle Dove and descends upon a flock of sparrows then it is a Sparrowhawk, and if it is a large raptor circling above the forest then it is a Goshawk. The Sparrowhawk and Goshawk, however, represent only a small fraction of what are known as birds of prey.

The Sparrowhawk is a common raptor in central Europe and most ornithologists are convinced that no other species of sparrowhawk lives or breeds here. Nevertheless, a bird slightly different from the Sparrowhawk is occasionally sighted or shot down in this area. It is a Levant Sparrowhawk that has strayed here from its breeding grounds in south-eastern Europe or southern Asia. It also nests in Africa south of the Sahara.

Closely related to the Sparrowhawk, the Levant Sparrowhawk is also very similar in appearance. It has longer, narrower wings and shorter tail, however, and the black wing tips stand out in sharp contrast to the light wing linings. The Sparrowhawk has a barred underside to the wing.

The nest is placed in trees in deciduous woods. It measures 25 to 35 centimetres across and the softly lined hollow contains two to four eggs, spotted green, blue, and brown. The young hatch after four to five weeks and abandon the nest at the age of forty-five days.

Red Kite

Milvus milvus

Accipitridae

In the introductory text, it was stated that raptors build their nests of branches of varying thickness and line them with dry grass, leaves, or moss. The Red Kite and its relative the Black Kite, however, line their nests with all kinds of industrial waste — bits of cloth, rubber, paper, bones, pieces of leather and fur, straw, plastic bags, wads of cotton, and even such things as woollen mittens or a school exercise book. It is hard to explain why they have such a liking for these things.

The Red Kite is slightly larger than the Buzzard. It measures 62 centimetres in length, weighs 1000 to 1250 grams and has a wingspan of 150 to 160 centimetres. The plumage has rufous tints, the head being a lighter colour with longitudinal streaks. Typical of the Red Kite is the deeply forked tail and light patches on the underside of the wings, which are angled in soaring flight. It can be distinguished from the Black Kite by the lighter, more rufous colour of the plumage and more deeply forked tail.

The Red Kite is found in the western Palaearctic. It makes its home and breeds in the northernmost parts of Africa, the Canary and Cape Verde islands, and Asia Minor. In Europe its range of distribution extends from the south across central Europe to southern Scandinavia and eastwards as far as the Ukraine. It is very rarely seen in Denmark, Belgium, and Holland, where it nests only occasionally, and is also absent in western Czechoslovakia. It is a migratory bird that winters mainly in the northern Mediterranean. The autumn flight south begins as early as August and most birds return to their nesting grounds in March.

Red Kite

continued

The Red Kite has a light, buoyant flight and is expert at soaring, making the most of the air currents. It feeds on the remains of prey left by other raptors or on carrion and refuse. It will also attack a small hare or small bird, but usually catches fieldmice, lizards, ground squirrels, moles, or larger insects in its flight just above the ground. It may also often be seen over water where it collects dead fishes from the surface. Its keen eyesight spots any carrion in the area.

The Red Kite nests at the forest edge or in small, isolated woodland groves. It may build its own nest high in the treetops but prefers to use the abandoned nests of crows or other birds. In April to May the female lays two to three whitish eggs spotted with brown, which she usually incubates alone for about thirty days; only rarely is she relieved by her mate. The young remain in the nest for about forty to forty-five days.

Black Kite

Milvus migrans

Accipitridae

The Black Kite shows a more marked inclination to food parasitism than does the Red Kite. Weighing almost 1 kilogram and with a wingspan of 145 to 155 centimetres, it has all the requirements for capturing animals even as large as a fowl but it prefers to feed on prey caught by other raptors. It has been known to harass an eagle unceasingly until the eagle released its hold on its victim, leaving it to the robber. Even its nesting habits are adapted to this method of obtaining food. The Black Kite frequently occupies abandoned nests in a heron or cormorant colony where it finds ample food in the form of dead fishes that fall to the ground from the nests when the adults feed their offspring. For the same reason it will settle near the nest of a falcon, Osprey, or Goshawk. It generally inhabits woodlands, not far from a river, lake, or the seashore, where it often catches live and dead fishes. When food is scarce, it will even eat lizards, frogs, insects, snails, and earthworms.

The Black Kite is about the size of the Buzzard and resembles it in colour. Its plumage is dark brown; adult birds have the head and breast coloured greyish white with dark, longitudinal streaks. There is no difference between the sexes except that the male is rather smaller. The Black Kite can be identified in flight by the slightly forked tail and the six outspread primaries (the Buzzard and Red Kite have only five). Moreover, the Black Kite has narrower wings than the Buzzard.

132

Black Kite

continued

The Black Kite occurs in eight geographical races practically throughout the whole of the Old World, being absent only in the northernmost parts of Europe and Asia. It is also found in Australia and the East Indies. In Europe, it inhabits lowlands and hilly country but is not seen in high mountains. After the young birds are fully grown, which is usually in August and September, it departs for its winter quarters in tropical and South Africa, returning to its nesting grounds again in late March or April.

Once built, the nest is used by a pair of birds for many years, being added on to every year and reaching a height of 25 to 80 centimetres and diameter of 50 to 100 centimetres. Both partners share the task of building. The nest is also added to, though to a lesser degree, during the nesting period, with both birds daily bringing a few fresh twigs with which they increase the height of the perimeter.

From late April to the beginning of May, the female lays two to three eggs which are very similar to those of the Red Kite. They are incubated mostly by the hen, though her mate helps occasionally. The young hatch one after the other in about thirty days. The youngest is usually cast aside and when it dies is eaten by its older siblings. The young birds leave the nest at the age of forty-two to forty-five days.

Black-shouldered Kite

Accipitridae

Elanus caeruleus

Vast park-like country with sparse woods in Africa, Madagascar, southern Asia, and southern Portugal is where the Black-shouldered Kite makes its home. It weighs approximately 230 grams and is about the size of a Kestrel. The plumage is grey-blue above and white on the underside with broad black shoulder patches. The short tail is slightly forked. Immature birds are greyish brown above and whitish tinged with rufous on the underside.

The long, pointed wings are clearly evident in flight. The Black-shouldered Kite is very good at soaring and when on the pursuit of its prey, may often be seen hovering in one spot like the Kestrel. It is not very plentiful in its area of distribution but wherever there is an abundance of food, such as where the locust population is large or a steppe fire has taken its toll, the Black-shouldered Kite congregates in large numbers. Besides insects, it eats small mammals, birds, lizards, and all kinds of refuse. Its voice is delicate and melodious.

The nest is built of slender branches close above the ground in trees and bushes. The clutch consists of three to five eggs spotted with reddish brown, which the female begins to incubate as soon as the first one is laid. European birds breed in Portugal in March to May. In tropical areas, nesting is determined by the climatic conditions. Incubation lasts twenty-five to twenty-six days and the young hatch at two- to three-day intervals, abandoning the nest thirty to forty days later in the same order as they hatched.

Swallow-tailed Kite

Accipitridae

Elanoides forficatus

In Europe, ornithologists sometimes come across a rare visitor from as far away as America, usually brought here by fierce gales that often carry birds thousands of kilometres. That is the explanation for the rare occurrence in Europe of the Swallow-tailed Kite, which is native to the area extending from the south-eastern United States to Argentina. In the early 1900s there have been two confirmed reports of Swallow-tailed Kites brought down in Germany; finds of further specimens are less trustworthy.

The Swallow-tailed Kite is an elegant, distinctively coloured bird with a deeply forked tail. It measures about 60 centimetres from the tip of its bill to the tip of the tail but actually it is smaller because the tail is practically as long as the body. Adults are white with black mantle, wings, and tail. Immatures have grey, finely spotted upper parts.

The Swallow-tailed Kite flies in graceful curves close to the ground in search of the small mammals, lizards, and birds and their young it feeds on. It is also skilled at catching flying insects with its claws and eating them on the wing. The nest is generally located high in the treetops. The clutch consists of two to three irregularly spotted eggs which the female lays between January and June, depending on the climatic conditions.

Osprey

Pandion haliaetus

Pandionidae

A bird that harpoons fish with its body — that is how this raptor might be described — and it lives almost exclusively on fishes. It flies in graceful curves above the water and as soon as it spies the dark shape of a fish it presses its wings close to its body and plunges feet first into the water from a height of 10 to 50 metres, emerging with its prey held fast in a crushing grip as it becomes airborne again with powerful strokes of its wings, even if its victim weighs as much as 2 kilograms. Immediately, it shakes the water out of its feathers and continues on with completely dry plumage, which is kept well oiled with the secretions of the developed uropygial gland at the base of the tail. The Osprey captures live as well as diseased and dead fishes. Its long, sharp, curved talons sink into the fish's back permitting no escape. With two toes in front and two at the back, the feet serve as an excellent vice. In addition, the undersides of the toes have pads with a rough, sandpaper-like surface which helps maintain a secure hold on the fish. When the waters in its hunting grounds are clouded then it also catches small mammals and birds, particularly young ones.

The Osprey has a dark, almost black back with white crown, white underside, and a dark band across the eye. The white belly probably plays an important role in hunting fishes for the bird is not as conspicuous against the bright background of the sky as one with dark underparts and thus is not as readily noticed by the fish. It weighs 1.5 to 2 kilograms and has a wingspan of up to 170 centimetres. Characteristic of the Osprey, apart from the coloration, is the flight silhouette with wings held slightly back in active flight. When soaring, however, the wings are spread out straight.

Osprey

continued

The Osprey breeds in the north and south of Europe, Asia, Australia, the Sunda Islands, North America, and Central America. In central Europe, however, it has been persecuted to such a degree that it has practically become extinct. At present the largest Osprey population is in Scandinavia where the birds are not subject to such persecution. In September or October, before the waters freeze over, the Osprey sets out for its wintering grounds in eastern, central, and southern Africa. Some birds remain in the Mediterranean region.

March to April is the period when the Osprey returns to its breeding grounds. Paired birds come back to the same nest for many years. Being repaired and added on to every year, such a nest may be as much as 1.5 metres across and 2.5 metres high. It is usually located in tall trees, sometimes also on high-tension electricity pylons; in the tundra the nest may even be placed on the ground. The two to three eggs, heavily spotted dark brown, are generally laid in May. The young hatch after thirty-seven to thirty-eight days and abandon the nest at the age of eight weeks.

Marsh Harrier

Accipitridae

Circus aeruginosus

Harriers comprise an unmistakable group of raptors. All four members of the group are graceful birds of prey that hunt small vertebrates and insects. They are slender-bodied, long-legged birds with long wings and tail, Around each eye is a ring of stiff feathers that forms a facial disc resembling that of owls.

The Marsh Harrier, which is the largest of the four and probably the most common, is perhaps the easiest harrier to identify. As in all harriers, there is a marked difference between the sexes (sexual dimorphism). The smaller male weighs between 400 and 720 grams and is coloured chestnut above with a yellowish head and breast and a reddish-brown belly. The tail is silvery grey and there are grey patches on the wings which in flight stand out in sharp contrast to the black wing tips. It lacks the white rump of the other harriers. The larger and heavier female (480 to 980 grams) and immature birds are entirely brown except for the head which is creamy white on the crown. The wingspan is 120 to 140 centimetres, that of the male always being the smaller.

The Marsh Harrier is widespread throughout all of Europe, except the extreme north, the whole of central Siberia, and eastward to the Far East. It also breeds in North Africa, Madagascar, and the Australian region. It is a migratory bird and leaves for its winter quarters in southern Europe and north-western and central Africa in late September, returning to its nesting grounds at the beginning of March.

Marsh Harrier

continued

It forages for food mostly by the edges of ponds, in overgrown inlets and oxbow lakes, in reed beds, and occasionally in open fields and marshes near water. In this type of country, it may be seen flying a slow, erratic course. It never seems to be a particularly good flier but it is worth remembering that its type of flight is ideally adapted to its way of life. The Marsh Harrier does not capture its prey on the wing but seeks it on the ground or on water. When it spies a frog resting on a stone, a fieldmouse, or a young bird swimming on the surface of a pond it swoops down upon its prey and grasps it with its long, thin, clawed toes.

The nest is placed in bent reeds in the thickest part of the reed bed, although sometimes it may rest directly on the water. The Marsh Harrier likes to occupy the old nests of water birds. In May the female lays three to six roundish, whitish eggs which are incubated for one month. The young, covered with white down, are fed a variety of animal foods and are capable of flight at the age of seven weeks.

Hen Harrier

Circus cyaneus

Accipitridae

All harriers have a long, slender body, emarginated wing tips, and a fairly long tail. They fly rather like a scrap of paper tossed by the wind. Characteristic of this group of raptors is that in flight, particularly when gliding or soaring, all hold their wings with the tips pointing slightly upwards forming an open V when viewed from the front or back.

The Hen Harrier is the largest of the three greyish harriers, though the differences in size between the adult birds of only a centimetre or so cannot be used as an identification feature in the field. The male weighs 330 to 400 grams, measures about 50 centimetres in length, and has a wingspan of 100 to 120 centimetres. The female may weigh as much as 500 grams. The male is plain ash-grey with a white rump which contrasts sharply with the black wing tips. It can be distinguished from the very similar Montagu's Harrier by the lack of black stripes on the wings and the unstreaked belly. Distinguishing between the females of these greyish coloured species, however, is difficult. They are brown above, and onion yellow streaked with brown on the underside. Juveniles have the same coloration as the females until they reach maturity.

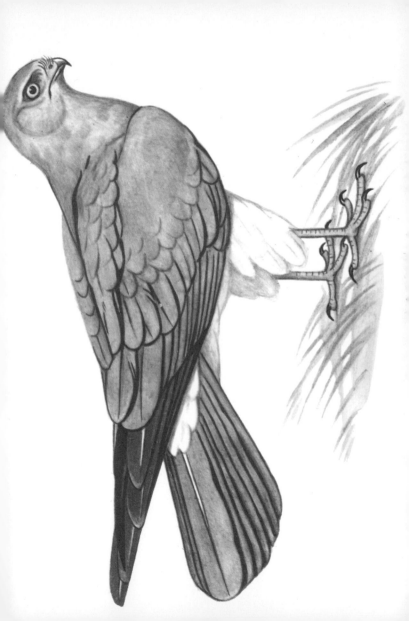

Hen Harrier

continued

The Hen Harrier nests near large ponds covered with reed beds and bordered with thick vegetation, beside oxbow lakes, in marshes, swampy meadows, and on moorlands. It often builds its nest among growing grain, in a warm forest clearing, or in open country; the nest is always placed on the ground. The Hen Harrier is distributed, though not abundantly, throughout practically all of Europe except for northern Scandinavia and central Siberia. It is also found in North America with the exception of the northernmost parts.

The Hen Harrier arrives on its nesting territory in March. The courtship display consists of beautiful aerial manoeuvres including various acrobatic feats. The simple nest of dry plant stalks and twigs, measuring 40 to 50 centimetres across, is built between April and June, usually by the female alone. The task takes several days. The whitish eggs, sometimes tinged with blue, are laid in the softly lined depression and incubated for thirty days. The four to six nestlings, covered with white down, are fed fieldmice, frogs, lizards, birds' eggs, and insects by the parents. After about thirty-five days the young are mature enough to leave the nest and fend for themselves.

Pallid Harrier

Accipitridae

Circus macrourus

The Pallid Harrier, which makes its home on the dry steppes of eastern Europe and western Siberia, is a rare visitor to central Europe, where it nests only very occasionally. It is grey in colour and measures 43 to 48 centimetres in length with a wingspan of 105 to 115 centimetres. The male's average weight is 330 grams, the female's 450 grams. It lacks the black bar on the wings but like the Hen Harrier, has black wing tips. The underside of its body is almost white as is the rump.

Just as difficult to identify is the differently coloured female, which is practically indistinguishable from the female Montagu's Harrier. She is brown above with yellowish, brown-streaked underparts. The juveniles can be distinguished from those of the Hen Harrier by the fact that their brown underparts are not streaked.

In central Europe the Pallid Harrier may be seen only from August to October and in spring in April or May, when it passes through on its way to and from its wintering grounds in central and South Africa. Siberian birds winter in India.

The habits of this harrier are very similar to those of the other species, though it prefers drier localities. The three to five whitish eggs, laid in May to June, are incubated for thirty days and the young abandon the nest thirty-five to forty-five days after hatching.

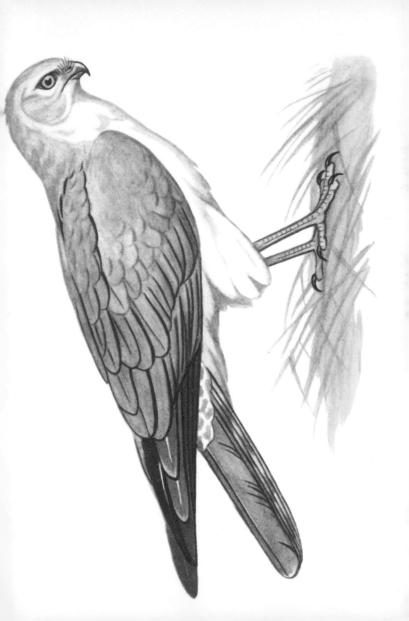

Montagu's Harrier

Accipitridae

Circus pygargus

Montagu's Harrier is the smallest of the three very similar greyish-blue harriers. It measures 41 to 46 centimetres, has a wingspan of 105 to 115 centimetres, and weighs 280 to 430 grams, about the same as an adult partridge. Here, too, the differently coloured female is larger and heavier than the male (weighing about 100 grams more). The adult male can be distinguished from the Hen and Pallid Harriers by the sharply defined black bar on its grey wings and blackish-brown streaks on the lighter underside. The female is brown above and yellow streaked with brown on the underside like the other female harriers. Juveniles resemble the female but lack the streaks on the breast and belly.

Harriers are so similar in appearance that it may be difficult to distinguish them. The following table sets out the main distinguishing features of the adult males of Hen, Montagu's, and Pallid Harriers. The Marsh Harrier has differently coloured plumage.

	rump	*throat*	*belly*	*wing bar*
Hen Harrier	glowing white	greyish blue	unstreaked	lacking
Montagu's Harrier	greyish blue	greyish blue	streaked	very marked
Pallid Harrier	whitish	white	unstreaked	lacking

Montagu's Harrier

continued

Montagu's Harrier is found throughout practically all of Europe, its range extending northwards as far as southern Scandinavia, southwards to North Africa (Morocco and Algeria), and eastwards to central Siberia, to the Altai Mountains, and the Sverdlovsk region. In Europe, however, it is not plentiful, nesting there only occasionally. It is more likely to be seen in Europe in late August and September, when it is en route to its winter quarters in the Mediterranean or northern Africa. It returns to its nesting grounds at the end of April and in May.

Montagu's Harrier frequents open, park-like country with ponds, scattered woods, fields and meadows, marshes, and moors and heaths. It is a bird of the lowlands and is never found in mountains at higher elevations.

Following their arrival at the breeding grounds, the birds commence their nuptial flights, the male's aerial display being exceptionally beautiful. Like a large, silvery gull he soars aloft, then plummets down towards the ground only to fly up again, making mock attacks, and continually circling around the female.

The nest is built by both partners in a dry spot on the ground, concealed by thick undergrowth. The first whitish eggs are laid at the beginning of May; the entire clutch consists of usually three to five but sometimes as many as ten eggs. The young hatch after thirty days and are fed small vertebrates by the parents. By the time they are thirty-five days old they are quite adept at flying.

Gyrfalcon

Falco rusticolus

A second unmistakable group of European raptors is the falcons. Characteristic of the family is the notch in the upper bill known as the 'tooth' of the falcon. This, of course, can serve to identify the bird only at close quarters. Identifying characteristics in the field are the flight pattern, the shape of the wings, and the flight silhouette.

All falcons have long, narrow, sickle-shaped wings with pointed tips, unlike eagles, buzzards, and vultures, which have emarginated wings.

Largest of the European falcons is the Gyrfalcon, which inhabits the northernmost parts of Scandinavia, mostly the tundra, although it is also found further south, particularly in the mountains of central Asia. It also occurs in the northern parts of North America. Gyrfalcons from more southerly regions are darker and smaller whereas birds of the far north are almost white and larger.

The Gyrfalcon is a noble bird, stronger, faster, more robust, bolder, and more daring even than the Peregrine Falcon. It measures 51 to 56 centimetres in length, weighs 1000 to 2000 grams, and has a wingspan of up to 130 centimetres. European birds have greyish or brownish upper parts and white, brown-spotted underside. They lack the moustachial streak. The Gyrfalcon nests on cliffs or on the ground, and the clutch consists of three to five eggs spotted with yellowish brown, which are incubated for twenty-eight to twenty-nine days mostly by the female. The young fledge at the age of forty-six to forty-nine days.

White Gyrfalcon

Falconidae

Falco rusticolus candicans

The White Gyrfalcon, almost pure white as its name suggests, and only slightly spotted, is found in northern Greenland and Canada. It is the northernmost race of the species and occurs only as a rare straggler in Europe. It hunts small birds but will also catch a duck, Capercaillie, Black Grouse, large gull, hare, and even an Arctic Fox. In the past its strength and boldness made it a popular bird for falconry. In medieval times, organized expeditions of falconers set out from the shores of Denmark for Greenland's rocky coasts to capture and bring back these magnificent white birds, both young and adults, which they trained for months before taking them out to hunt.

Falcons and eagles, however, are few in number and the Goshawk is the bird generally used for falconry today. Once, hunters rode out to hunt on horseback with hooded falcons perched on their gloved wrists. When the hunter spotted his prey he removed the leather hood and cast the falcon up into the air. The falcon overtook the flying bird, forced it to the ground, and landed on top, being relieved of its victim within seconds by the hunter who quickly rode to the spot on his horse.

Peregrine Falcon

Falco peregrinus

Falconidae

The Peregrine is widely distributed, occurring in about twenty different geographical races throughout the world. It is becoming increasingly rare in Europe, however, and in some countries it has disappeared altogether; in others only a few pairs nest on cliff ledges, in trees, and in the towers of castle ruins. The bird has a wingspan of about 1 metre and the male is about a third smaller and lighter than the female, which weighs as much as 1300 grams. The upper side of both sexes is slate grey, the underside light with black barring. There is a moustachial streak from the base of the bill to the throat.

The Peregrine Falcon hunts its prey exclusively on the wing, never attacking a victim on the ground. In rapid flight, when diving to attack, it attains speeds of 270 to 320 kilometres per hour. It does not attack birds flying in closed formations but only single individuals, often attempting to separate one from the flock. Birds in flight will often fend off an attack by closing ranks as soon as they notice a falcon or by plummeting to the ground like a stone.

When the Peregrine sees a potential victim it tries to get above it. Its large, powerful wings enable it to overtake a bird a kilometre distant within a very short time. Observations have shown that a Peregrine can cover a distance of 600 metres during the time it takes a pigeon to fly 200 metres. When it has almost overtaken its prey it halts and plunges down upon it from above with wings pressed close to the body. Flying slightly below its victim, it then swerves up again to sink its talons into the bird's body. The long talon on the hind toe generally penetrates deepest. A small bird is easily carried away in the Peregrine's grasp but larger birds, such as a duck, are only pierced with the talons and struck to the ground.

Peregrine Falcon

continued

The Peregrine usually takes domestic and wild doves, starlings, crows, Rooks, Jays, and Lapwings. Wild game comprises only about 5 per cent of its entire diet.

Usually in April (in the north in May or June) the female lays three to four eggs, with brownish-red and yellow spots, on the ground or in a disused nest. Both parents take turns incubating for twenty-eight to twenty-nine days. Unlike other raptors the male also shares the duties of feeding the young, which fledge at the age of thirty-six to forty days. Young Peregrines from Europe migrate south-west for the winter, adult birds remain in their nesting grounds but roam far afield.

Lanner Falcon

Falco biarmicus

Falconidae

The Lanner's main area of distribution is Africa, whence it extends to southern Italy, the Balkans, Asia Minor, and Arabia. It is found in bare rocky places, such as karst scenery, in deep gorges laced with rock masses, and in upland plateaus.

Here it finds plenty of prey such as Jackdaws, Rock Doves, and other birds that nest in the rock cavities. A pair of birds usually works as a team in hunting prey. The Lanner Falcon perches on cliff ledges on the lookout for prey; at other times it takes advantage of the rocky terrain concealing itself behind ledges as it flies in search of food, catching its unsuspecting prey by surprise. Unlike the Peregrine it does not strike it on the ground but on the wing, carrying its prey off to a regularly visited spot where it proceeds to devour the flesh.

The Lanner is similar to the Peregrine in shape and size, measuring 45 centimetres in length, weighing 500 to 900 grams and possessing a wingspan of about 105 centimetres. The male and female are much alike in appearance except that the male is slightly smaller. The upper side of the body is slate grey with rufous and grey bands, the nape is yellow and the underside is white and finely spotted. Information about its breeding habits is fragmentary and incomplete. The nest is placed on cliffs. The clutch consists of three to four brown-marbled eggs laid in February in more southerly regions, elsewhere in March. The incubation period is about twenty-eight days and the young abandon the nest after five to six weeks.

Saker Falcon

Falco cherrug

Falconidae

The Saker Falcon is not a typical aerial hunter and mammals form a greater part of its diet. Its methods of hunting are more varied. It attacks slower-flying and less agile birds plunging down upon them from the sky, but more usually takes advantage of the landscape, exploiting the element of surprise to capture skilfully the bird or mammal with sharp twists and turns. When performing these manoeuvres, it makes good use of its relatively long tail, which it fans out to brake or change direction. In its hunting grounds it has several regularly used vantage points from which it attacks ground squirrels, hares, marmots, and partridges. Often it circles in the air like the Buzzard, sometimes hovering in one spot on the lookout for prey. Measuring about 50 centimetres in length, weighing 800 to 1200 grams, and possessing a wingspan of 105 to 120 centimetres, it attacks even larger animals such as ducks, small bustards, harriers, and owls.

The male and female have similar plumage — brown back and white underside with brown spots. The Saker Falcon is found in south-eastern Europe and central Asia. It usually nests in trees, rarely on cliffs. The entire clutch comprises four to five brown-spotted eggs which are incubated for about thirty days, usually by the female alone. The young fledge at the age of forty-one to forty-five days.

Eleonora's Falcon

Falco eleonorae

The period of the growth and rearing of the young of a species must be at a time when there is a plentiful supply of food, because otherwise the existence of the young and of the entire species would be threatened. Most birds begin breeding in spring so that their offspring will hatch when there is plenty of animal or vegetable food for them to eat. Some birds, however, nest at a more unusual time. Eleonora's Falcon breeds on the rocky islands and shores of the Mediterranean, laying its two to three reddish-brown spotted eggs on cliffs. It does not begin nesting until mid-summer, either at the end of July or beginning of August, that is, at a time when the young of other birds of prey are already fully grown or are learning to fend for themselves. Eleonora's Falcon, however, waits until the insects are plentiful and when large numbers of small birds stop to rest on the rocky shores on their way to their winter homes in the heart of Africa.

Eleonora's Falcon is intermediate in size between the Hobby and the Peregrine. It has a wingspan of 90 to 100 centimetres and occurs in two colour phases. The dark phase is mostly brownish black with yellow eye rim; in the light phase it has a white throat patch and rufous-brown, streaked underside.

Hobby

Falco subbuteo

In late summer the reed beds of large ponds fill with swarms of birds. Every evening flocks of Swallows, Starlings, and other birds converge there from all sides to roost among the thick reeds which afford excellent protection. Such roosting places are well known to the Hobby, which visits them regularly for its food. If the Hobby's first attempt is not successful, it does not give up but perches on a nearby tree and patiently waits until another group of birds arrives to spend the night. Then, it dashes to the attack and tries to separate a single bird from the group. Taken by surprise, the victim has practically no hope of escape. The Hobby is a very skilled and fast flier which, even in gliding flight, attains a speed of 150 kilometres per hour and in attack 240 kilometres an hour, easily overtaking even such rapid fliers as Swallows and Swifts. Should the Hobby's first thrust miss its mark then it quickly flies up again and soon closes the gap between it and its prey, that is, unless the intended victim has not concealed itself on the ground or in the undergrowth.

This method of obtaining food influenced the shape of the body, which has perfect aerodynamic lines, and the wings, which are long, narrow, and pointed. The shape of a modern jet aircraft is not dissimilar to a Hobby.

In shape and colouring the Hobby looks like a small Peregrine. It has a wingspan of up to 80 centimetres. The upper side of its body is slate grey; the underside is light with dark streaks. It has a well-defined moustachial streak and rufous legs. Both sexes are alike except in size, the male being somewhat smaller than the female.

Hobby

continued

The Hobby is found throughout practically all of Europe, except for the northernmost parts, in the temperate regions of Asia, and in north Africa. It winters in southern Africa and southern Asia, leaving its nesting grounds in October and returning again in April. It prefers open country with fields, meadows, and scattered woodlands.

It nests in trees, generally using the abandoned nests of other birds. A complete clutch consists of two to four eggs spotted with brownish red. They are incubated for twenty-eight days, usually by the female alone, and the young abandon the nest when they are twenty-eight to thirty-two days old.

Merlin

Falco columbarius

Falconidae

In medieval days, when falconry was at its peak, wild game was not only hunted by wealthy feudal lords but often also by their ladies. When trained birds of prey were used, however, the men would ride with larger and heavier ones such as falcons or eagles whereas the ladies used smaller, lighter birds that would not tire them as much. The Merlin, smallest of the European falcons, was often used for this purpose. It weighs a mere 170 to 200 grams and has a wingspan of 60 to 70 centimetres, but it could easily be used for hunting birds as large as a goose. Lacking the strength to kill the victim itself, nevertheless, the Merlin was able to bring it to the ground, where the goose was then easy prey for the hunters. Even in the wild, however, the Merlin, flying fast low over the ground, attacks birds as large as a Blackbird or woodpecker.

The Merlin is found in northern Europe, Asia, and North America north of the United States. The southern boundary of its range in Asia runs through southern Siberia. It inhabits mostly tundras and forest tundras; in central Asia it occurs also high in the mountains. In central Europe it may be seen mainly in the autumn months on its passage to its wintering grounds in western and southern Europe, north Africa, and southern Asia. With the arrival of March it is back again in its breeding grounds, beginning preparations for nesting.

Merlin

continued

The nest is generally located on the ground, either on cliff ledges or on some elevated spot, less frequently in trees at a height of about 10 metres. Sometimes, the Merlin will also use an abandoned nest of some other bird. The nest is a haphazard structure of twigs and plants gathered in the immediate vicinity.

The whitish eggs are so thickly covered with chocolate-brown spots that the ground colour is completely concealed. The first egg is laid some time in May and the others at two-day intervals. When the nest contains four to five, sometimes as many as seven eggs, the female starts incubating, being relieved occasionally by her mate. The young hatch after twenty-eight to thirty-two days and are fed by the female alone. Only later does the male also help with the feeding. The young birds leave the nest when they are about twenty-five to twenty-seven days old; if the nest is placed on the ground then they scatter in the vicinity a few days earlier.

The male has slate-grey upper parts with a reddish patch on the nape. The grey tail has a broad black band near the tip. The underside is rufous and heavily streaked. The female and juveniles have a brown back, brown-striped tail, and whitish underside with brown streaks.

Red-footed Falcon

Falconidae

Falco vespertinus

The beautifully coloured Red-footed Falcon flies buoyantly in flocks near the ground catching large insects in the air with its sharp talons. This small falcon with a wingspan of about 75 centimetres feeds mainly on insects but it may acquire something larger by harassing a Kestrel, for example, until it gives up its prey.

The Red-footed Falcon breeds in Hungary, also inhabiting steppes, forest-steppes, and cultivated steppes with scattered trees in eastern Europe, central Siberia, and eastern Asia. Occasionally, it also nests in Austria, Czechoslovakia, and Poland. Its diet forces it to set out in September in search of insects to places as far distant as east and southern Africa, from where it returns to its breeding grounds in April.

The male is slate grey with red feet and under-tail coverts. The female has a bluish-grey upper side streaked with black, a dark moustachial streak, cinnamon head, and rufous underside.

The Red-footed Falcon nests in trees, usually in the abandoned nests of other birds. It often forms colonies of as many as a hundred pairs. The eggs resemble those of the Kestrel, being only slightly smaller. The three to five young nestlings hatch after about twenty-three days of incubation and leave the nest after four weeks.

Lesser Kestrel

Falco naumanni

Falconidae

Identifying kestrels in northern Europe is a simple matter because generally the only one to be found there is the Kestrel. In Spain, Italy, Austria, the Balkans, and south-eastern Europe, however, other kestrels can be found, and in particular the Lesser Kestrel. It is slightly smaller than the Kestrel, being about 30 centimetres long and with a wingspan of 65 centimetres, but otherwise it is very similar. The male lacks the black spots on the back and has a greyish-blue band on the wings. The females of both species are practically indistinguishable. Besides Europe, the Lesser Kestrel is also found in the northernmost belt of Africa and in central Asia.

It inhabits open country — steppes and forest steppes — and may be found even near human habitations as well as in absolutely barren land. Whole colonies of nesting birds may be seen in clay banks, cliffs, and even villages. Sometimes, these colonies comprise only a few, at other times as many as a hundred pairs, all of which find adequate food within a fairly small range. They catch mainly locusts, grasshoppers, beetles, butterflies, and other flying insects, but will also eat small vertebrates.

Lesser Kestrels return from their winter quarters in Africa in March and April or May, the time when the female lays three to six, brown-marbled eggs which she and her mate take turns incubating for twenty-eight to twenty-nine days. At the age of thirty days the young birds abandon the nest and at the end of September they depart for their winter homes.

Kestrel

Falco tinnunculus

Falconidae

The Kestrel is the most common and widespread of the falcons. It may be found in all types of habitats, but mostly in open agricultural country with scattered groves. Before breeding, it seeks out an old crow's or magpie's nest in which it lays four to seven brown-marbled eggs in April to May. At this time the male's call notes may often be heard as he flies in circles round the nest during his courtship display. The Kestrel also commonly nests on cliffs, in various cavities and castle ruins, as well as on buildings in towns. As soon as the female begins incubating she is kept supplied with food by the male. The young hatch after about twenty-nine days, being fed mostly by the female, rarely by the male, though he continues to supply the entire family with food as his mate very rarely leaves the nest to hunt. When the young birds reach the age of twenty-eight to thirty-two days they abandon the nest and venture forth on independent flights in the neighbourhood.

The Kestrel is distributed throughout Europe, Asia, and Africa, where it occurs in about fifteen races. Some birds remain in their breeding grounds throughout the year, flying to the Mediterranean only in severe winters.

The Kestrel's reddish back is readily identified even in flight. The male's has black spots, the female's is barred. The male has a grey head and long grey tail with a broad, subterminal black band. The female has a rufous, heavily barred tail. The underside in both sexes is creamy white and streaked.

Kestrel

continued

A very good means of identifying the Kestrel is its hovering flight. The Sparrowhawk, which is about the same size, never does this. Besides, the Kestrel has longer and sharply pointed wings measuring about 75 centimetres from wing tip to wing tip.

A hovering Kestrel is on the lookout for food. With head down it surveys the ground for any sign of movement. If it sees nothing it flies to another spot a short distance away and again hovers in a single spot. When it sights prey it closes its wings and plummets downward, spreading them just above the ground to brake its descent but still striking the unsuspecting fieldmouse with great force, breaking its back with its beak and proceeding to devour its flesh. It requires three fieldmice daily to satisfy its appetite. The Kestrel also catches other small vertebrates and larger insects, but fieldmice, mice, and ground squirrels make up as much as 86 per cent of its diet.

OWLS

Scops Owl

Strigidae

Otus scops

If you were to place the Eagle Owl, the largest of the European owls, the medium-large Long-eared Owl, and the small Scops Owl side by side you would discover that all three are surprisingly similar in shape and colouring. The Eagle Owl, however, measures about 60 centimetres in length whereas the Scops Owl is only 19 centimetres long. Despite their superficial similarity each of these owls belongs to a different genus.

The Scops Owl is a rare visitor to central Europe, its regular breeding grounds being the warmer areas of southern Europe, north Africa, and Asia Minor. From eastern Europe its range extends as far as western Siberia. It is a migratory bird and the only European owl that flies to central Africa in early autumn, returning again in March or April.

Its whistling call, monotonously repeated at two-second intervals, may be heard in open woodlands on warm nights. If you are lucky you may even catch a glimpse of its dark silhouette. It is rarely seen, however, in the daytime when it conceals itself in cavities or thick branches. Its protective grey-brown coloration makes it look like the dry stump of a branch.

The four to six eggs are laid in a tree hollow, rock crevice, or old nest of some other bird and are incubated for twenty-four to twenty-five days by the female alone. The young leave the nest at the age of twenty-eight days, learning to hunt insects, small lizards, and birds as their parents do.

Pygmy Owl

Strigidae

Glaucidium passerinum

In late September, when the Red Deer rut is at its height in Europe's forests, their trumpeting is the only noticeable sound to break the stillness of the early morning or evening. The waiting hunter is occasionally surprised by a series of soft, melodious whistles, sometimes on a rising scale ending in a trill. They sound from various places and various heights and only the experienced hunter realizes that only an owl is capable of flying among the branches without making a sound. Even so, he may sometimes be confused by such a pleasing note, for most owls produce harsher cries.

This autumn songster is the Pygmy Owl which, being no bigger than the Starling, is the smallest European owl. The upper side of its body is dark brown with white spots, the underside greyish white with dark, horizontal vermiculation. The facial disc is not very distinct because it consists of several dark concentric circles. When perching, the Pygmy Owl jerks its grey-and-white striped tail from side to side.

It is found in the coniferous forests of northern Europe, its range extending from there in a narrow belt far into eastern Asia. It occurs locally also in certain mountains in central and southern Europe. The four to eight eggs are laid in tree cavities in April or May and are incubated for about twenty-eight days. Despite its small size, the Pygmy Owl is able to catch sparrows, tits, finches, and mice. If food is plentiful it stores it for the future in tree cavities.

Little Owl

Athene noctua

Strigidae

The Little Owl is common in open country with scattered hedges and trees. It may be seen in parks, gardens, cemeteries, avenues, and copses, but it avoids extensive woodlands. It is widely distributed throughout north Africa, a large part of Europe, and Asia as far as northern China, Turkestan, northern India, and northern Iraq.

The Little Owl is about the size of a Turtle Dove, weighing approximately 140 grams and with a wingspan of 50 centimetres. Its brown back is spotted with white and the light underside covered with dark longitudinal markings. The yellow eyes are practically concealed by the low, prominent 'eyebrows', and the facial disc is composed of fairly short feathers.

The Little Owl may be seen during the daytime, but it is more likely to be seen at dusk when it sets out to hunt. During the day it usually rests on branches, in hollows in walls, tree cavities, and similar places. When small birds discover its hiding place they drive it out and give chase to the accompaniment of loud cries as the Little Owl flies off in jerky, undulating flight trying to escape its pursuers. When its hiding place is approached by a human it bobs up and down. This is a mark of its agitation but at the same time it helps the owl to focus its eyes on the approaching figure.

The Little Owl is fairly common and may be seen near almost every village, where its call is well known. The flute-like call note, which may often be heard in spring from cemeteries, was believed by people to be calling them there, and the Little Owl was often thought to presage the death of the sick. In flight, it often utters barking notes, though it is also capable of emitting other, very unpleasant cries.

Little Owl

continued

The pellets that the Little Owl regurgitates are coloured grey and measure about 5 centimetres in length and 1 to 1.5 centimetres across. They contain the indigestible remains of fieldmice, mice, shrews, birds, amphibians, and insects. About 89 per cent of the vertebrates identified were harmful rodents. If you consider that a single fieldmouse can ruin as much as 1 kilogram of grain in a year, then you can understand how useful the Little Owl is.

The Little Owl does not build a nest. It lays its eggs in tree hollows, wall cavities, nestboxes, and occasionally even in rabbit holes. The breeding season, accompanied by its special 'song', begins in March and continues sometimes until May. In April and May the female is already incubating her clutch of four to five white eggs. The young are hatched after twenty-six to twenty-eight days and are fed by both parents until they leave the nest at the age of four to five weeks.

The Little Owl is a resident bird that stays the winter; only immatures are inclined to roam afield, sometimes even quite far from where they were born.

Tengmalm's Owl

Strigidae

Aegolius funereus

The deep coniferous forests of northern Europe, Asia, and North
America as well as the mountainous regions of central Europe are
the home of the small Tengmalm's Owl, which measures about
25 centimetres in length, and is very similar in appearance to the
Little Owl. Its plumage looks darker than that of the Little Owl, and
the immatures are definitely dark. The crown is spotted white
whereas that of the Little Owl is striped. The head appears to be
large because of the round facial disc which serves as a sound
reflector. The legs are thickly covered with feathers to the talons.
When hunting in the dark, Tengmalm's Owl uses primarily its
sense of hearing to locate its prey. Its keen hearing is improved still
further by the facial disc and the asymmetrically placed ears.

Tengmalm's Owl is a comparatively rare owl leading
a secretive life in the forest. During the day, it perches in the thick
branches waiting until dark to hunt. In spring and sometimes
even in autumn, it makes its presence known by its trisyllabic call
which is similar to the Hoopoe's. Unlike the Little Owl, which has
an undulating flight, it flies in a straight course.

It does not build a nest of its own but uses the cavities of trees or
old woodpecker's nests. In April to May the female lays four to six
white eggs in the unlined hollow. She incubates alone for twenty-
five to thirty-one days. The young leave the cavity after thirty
days but continue to be fed by the parents for some time.

Eagle Owl

Strigidae

Bubo bubo

The Eagle Owl is the largest European owl. The male weighs 2 to 3 kilograms, the female 3 to 3.5 kilograms and the wingspan measures 160 to 180 centimetres. It has the characteristic coloration of all owls. Distinctive are the large, glowing orange eyes, and ear tufts that look like horns.

A solitary bird, it does not associate with others of its kind. This is because of the Eagle Owl's food requirements whereby a large number of individuals in a limited area would lead to competition. That is why the Eagle Owl has such a scattered distribution throughout its range, which extends from north Africa through Europe (except for Britain) to central Asia and the Far East, and why the individual nests are located far apart.

The Eagle Owl is found mostly in wooded areas with steep rocks where it rears its young. It also occurs in lowland and mountain regions. Sometimes it nests even in tree cavities and castle ruins.

It hunts only at night, catching its prey both in the air and on the ground. It has keen eyesight and sense of hearing. Its hunting grounds cover an area of up to 70 square kilometres. Analysis of regurgitated pellets, which are 10 to 14 centimetres long and 3 to 4 centimetres thick, revealed that the Eagle Owl hunts everything from a fieldmouse or wren to a hare, Roe Deer, heron, Capercaillie or Goshawk. It will strike down even medium-sized raptors and owls. Even badgers, foxes, cats, hedgehogs; ducks, buzzards, and falcons have fallen prey to this enormous owl.

Eagle Owl

continued

The Eagle Owl is often harassed by diurnal birds, but only in the daytime. Hunters take advantage of this fact and use a tame owl to catch crows, magpies, and other birds. An owl is tethered by its feet to a T-shaped bar in an open space while the hunter hides in a nearby shelter and waits. As soon as flying birds notice the Eagle Owl, they set up a great hue and cry and immediately descend to the attack, completely forgetting their usual vigilance, making themselves easy targets. It often happens that birds shot down in this way include rare and protected raptors and the method is already prohibited in many countries.

The Eagle Owl's deep, pleasant call is most often heard during the courting season, which begins shortly after the birds return to their nesting sites in December and January. Paired birds occupy the same breeding territory for many years. The two to four white eggs are laid in a hollow, which has practically no lining, in late March and April. The young are hatched, covered with pale down, after thirty-five days and are fed by both parents. When they are seven weeks old they leave the nest even though they are not yet very good at flying.

Snowy Owl

Nyctea scandiaca

Strigidae

Birds of prey, and owls in particular, play an important role in controlling the numbers of fieldmice and mice, because these small rodents form the mainstay of their diet. Lemmings, large rodents of the northern tundras about the size of a mole, influence the yearly populations of the Snowy Owl which is almost as large and strong as the Eagle Owl.

The white plumage is only lightly spotted black; some older owls are almost pure white. It is found along the coastline of northern Europe, Asia, and North America and on islands in the Arctic Ocean. Sometimes it strays as far south as central and southern Europe.

The nest is located on the ground and the four to six eggs are laid in April to June. When the lemming population is large, attaining peak proportions every four years, the clutch contains as many as twelve eggs. When the lemming population is small the Snowy Owl lays fewer eggs or does not nest at all. A similar phenomenon — that is adaptation of the nesting habits to the food conditions — is found in the Buzzard.

The female begins incubating as soon as the first egg is laid and the first offspring is hatched after about thirty-four days. Because the eggs are laid at two-day intervals the difference between the first and last young to hatch may be as much as twenty days in the case of a clutch comprising ten eggs. The young are reared in the nest a long time — fifty to sixty days. An adult owl consumes one to four lemmings a day. An entire family consumes at least 1500 lemmings in two months.

Great Grey Owl

Strix nebulosa

Owls, particularly the larger species, are robust, heavy, powerful birds and the large, rounded head makes them seem even more so. This impression is emphasized by the thick coat of long, soft feathers. This applies also to the Great Grey Owl, which inhabits the coniferous forests and tundras of northern Europe, Asia, and North America. It is about the same size as the Eagle Owl (about 70 centimetres long) and has a wingspan of 130 to 140 centimetres. Comparison of the weight of the Great Grey Owl with that of the equally large Spotted Eagle reveals a marked difference. The male weighs about 750 grams and the female 1000 to 1200 grams, whereas the Spotted Eagle weighs two to three times as much.

The Great Grey Owl's plumage resembles old, lichen-covered bark. The upper side is marbled brown, grey, and white, and the underside is whitish streaked with brown. The strikingly small, yellow eyes are set in a bold, concentrically barred facial disc and there is a conspicuous black 'chin' below the beak.

The Great Grey Owl is a resident bird, flying south to southern Scandinavia, sometimes even to central Europe, only when lack of food demands it. In April to May it lays four to five eggs either in the old nest of other large birds or on the ground. It feeds on small mammals, mostly fieldmice, shrews and lemmings, though it also hunts small- and medium-sized birds.

Ural Owl

Strix uralensis

Strigidae

The Ural Owl inhabits the northern parts of Europe and forested areas of Siberia as far as Sakhalin and Japan; it occurs locally also in the Alps, Carpathians, Balkans, and the Bohemian Forest, so that it may be seen more often in central Europe than the Great Grey Owl.

The Ural Owl is about 60 centimetres long, has a wingspan of up to 120 centimetres and resembles the Tawny Owl. It is coloured greyish white or yellowish white streaked with brown. Like the Tawny Owl, it has black-brown eyes and often occurs in a grey as well as brown phase. The long, dark-striped tail is clearly visible in flight.

Its method of hunting is not very different from that of other northern owls. As a rule, it hunts at dusk but is often active also in daytime. Its diet consists chiefly of small mammals, mostly rodents, though when food is short it will also catch a young hare or birds as large as a pheasant or the Black Grouse.

It frequents all types of woods and nests either in spacious cavities or in the abandoned nests of other raptors. In March to April, the female lays three to four eggs, beginning to incubate as soon as the first is laid. The young hatch after twenty-seven to twenty-nine days and are tended by the parents a further five weeks.

Long-eared Owl

Asio otus

The Long-eared Owl, measuring only 34 to 36 centimetres in length, resembles the Eagle Owl in shape and coloration. When it sits motionless, the rufous-yellow plumage with dark-brown, tree-like, herringbone markings gives it the appearance of a dry stump of a branch with cracked bark. The likeness to a broken branch is emphasized by the long ear tufts. When danger threatens, the owl improves its camouflage by holding itself erect and pressing its feathers close to its body. The large eyes are orange or orange yellow.

The Long-eared Owl nests throughout most of Europe, in central Siberia, northern Africa, and North America. It may be found in forests of all kinds. During the daytime it remains concealed among thick branches with only the pile of pellets below its perch revealing its presence. The pellets are coloured grey and are 4 to 7.5 centimetres long and 2 to 3 centimetres thick. They are much more symmetrical than those of the Tawny Owl. Analysis of the pellets reveals the Long-eared Owl's food preferences. It consumes as many as six small mammals a day and it has been estimated that in one year it kills about 2000 fieldmice, mice, and other small vertebrates. A family of these owls consumes eighteen to twenty small mammals daily which, if rodents are few, equals 0.5 to 1 per cent of the population of small mammals on an area of about 5 square kilometres, which is the extent of the Long-eared Owl's hunting grounds. Analysis of the pellets reveals that fieldmice and mice make up 90 to 95 per cent of the bird's diet.

Long-eared Owl

continued

Availability of food has a marked influence on the owls' seasonal migrations. When there is plenty of food they remain in their territory but when fieldmice are few they roam the countryside or travel greater distances, usually in a south-westerly direction. Such flights are generally made in larger groups.

During courtship in spring, the Long-eared Owl's lengthy, repeated, hooting song may be heard. The courtship display consists of a rocking nuptial flight during which the male now and then claps his wings noisily together.

The Long-eared Owl does not build a nest of its own but uses the old nests of crows, magpies, or squirrels. The eggs may be laid as early as March but April or May is the more usual time. The clutch consists of four to six eggs which the female begins incubating as soon as the first is laid. The male does not assist in this task but brings her food, continuing to do so for the whole family when the young hatch, because the female does not leave the nest at all for the first few days. The young birds hatch after twenty-seven to twenty-eight days and can be distinguished from the offspring of the Tawny Owl and Barn Owl by the orange eyes and later also by the ear tufts. They abandon the nest at the age of twenty-four to twenty-six days.

Short-eared Owl

Asio flammeus

Strigidae

The Short-eared Owl is similar in plumage to the Long-eared Owl, but it is largely diurnal. It has a similar, but paler, colouring, and is about 4 centimetres longer, with a wingspan of about 1 metre, but its ear tufts are very short. It can be distinguished from the Long-eared Owl by the paler coloration, yellow eyes, and longitudinal streaks on the underside that lack the branch-like effect of the Long-eared Owl's.

The Short-eared Owl inhabits plains, marshes, and tundras throughout most of Europe, northern Asia, north and south Africa, North America, and the central parts of South America. Unlike other owls, it builds a nest on the ground among reeds, grass, or field crops. In hunts small mammals, mainly in the daytime. Its striking courtship display also takes place during the day. The four to seven eggs are laid in April to May and are incubated by the female alone for twenty-seven to twenty-eight days. The young leave the nest after seventeen days but are not able to fly until they are four weeks old.

Tawny Owl

Strix aluco

Strigidae

The Tawny Owl is the most common and widespread European owl. It is found in both coniferous and deciduous woods, parks, gardens, and sometimes even in villages, in hill and lowland country. Its range includes almost all of Europe (except for the northernmost areas), north-western Africa, and parts of Asia.

It is easily identified by the dark brown eyes. All other owls, except for the Ural Owl and Barn Owl which has a distinct, heart-shaped facial pattern, however, have yellow or orange eyes. The Tawny Owl occurs in two colour phases — grey and brown. It is interesting to note that even young birds from the same nest may be differently coloured. The owl's simple, greyish-white or brownish-white, bark-like plumage serves as excellent camouflage in the treetops where it rests during the day.

The Tawny Owl stays in its breeding grounds throughout the year, beginning preparations for nesting as early as February, when its call may also be heard. The female's call is rather shrill resembling the Little Owl's; the male's is a long, drawn-out hooting.

The Tawny Owl nests in various cavities, mainly tree hollows, also in large nestboxes and, if need be, even on the ground. The white eggs are laid in the bottom of the unlined cavity. A full clutch comprises three to four, sometimes six to seven eggs and is usually complete by March. The female incubates alone, starting as soon as the first or second egg is laid, the young hatching in succession. She only occasionally leaves the nest for a short time.

Tawny Owl

continued

The young hatch after twenty-eight days and are thickly covered with pale down. For the first ten days they are continually watched over by the female which feeds them food brought by the male. During this time she sees to it that the nest is kept clean by swallowing her offspring's faeces and regurgitated pellets.

When feeding the young, she first tears the flesh into smaller pieces. She does so with closed eyes, feeling the prey with the tactile feathers at the base of the beak. This phenomenon may be observed also in adult owls when they feed. They close their eyes and feel the prey, which they hold in their talons, with the bill and tactile feathers at its base, and only then do they start to eat it beginning with the head. This is because, being long-sighted, they are unable to focus their eyes properly on objects that are close up. The young leave the nest at the age of twenty-eight to thirty-six days but are not fully independent for some time.

The pellets regurgitated by the Tawny Owl are grey, 4 to 6 centimetres long, and 2 to 3 centimetres thick, and quite asymmetrical. They reveal that the owl's diet comprises about 70 per cent harmful rodents, 14 per cent birds, 11 per cent amphibians, and about 5 per cent insects. The owl's daily food requirements are the equal in weight of three fieldmice. Some years, however, fieldmice and mice comprise more than 90 per cent of the owl's catch.

Barn Owl

Strigidae

Tyto alba

Many ghost stories are probably derived from the fact that man could find no explanation for various night-time voices, cries, and other noises. People with a knowledge of wildlife and nature knew that the terrible snoring sounds and shrieks at night were made by the courting Barn Owl.

The Barn Owl is the loveliest European owl. It is about 34 centimetres long (about the same size as the Wood Pigeon) and the only owl with a heart-shaped facial disc. The underside is a light creamy white or rufous brown, sometimes even pure white, and the facial disc is always the same colour as the breast. The underparts are never streaked but only dotted with a few dark specks. The upper side of the body is rufous yellow with grey vermiculation. The fairly long legs, which resemble the letter X when the owl is perching, are feathered down to the claws.

The Barn Owl occurs in thirty-three different races in all of Europe, a large part of Asia, Indonesia, Australia, South America, and also in some parts of North America. Originally an inhabitant of rocky country where it nested in rock crevices, it may now be found in villages and towns nesting in attics, church steeples, castle towers, as well as in barns and haylofts. Life is easier for the owl here because human habitations afford a plentiful food supply in the form of mice, fieldmice, and small birds. It plays an extremely beneficial role in that it hunts harmful rodents. These comprise 70 per cent of the owl's diet. The Barn Owl requires three to four mice daily. It also catches a great many House Sparrows in attics and granaries. The pellets regurgitated by the owl are black and smooth on the surface, as if coated with a fine film of asphalt, fairly large (3.5 to 8 centimetres long and about 3 centimetres thick), and rounded at the tip.

Barn Owl

continued

The relationship between the food conditions and the Barn Owl's breeding habits is interesting. As a rule it nests once a year, under eaves. The three to six, sometimes even more, white eggs are laid in April or May and are incubated by the female for thirty to thirty-four days. The young are capable of flight after about fifty to sixty days. When food is plentiful the Barn Owl lays a greater number of eggs or else has two broods a year. It will nest even in the autumn. When food is scarce it usually does not nest at all.

Hawk Owl

Surnia ulula

Strigidae

Central Europe is sometimes visited by the Hawk Owl of the northern forests, which is about as large as the Tawny Owl. Its yellow eyes, resembling those of the Sparrowhawk, peer out of the well-defined facial mask which is almost white and ringed with a black band. The upper side of its body is black-brown streaked with white, and the underside has vermiculation similar to the Sparrowhawk's. The falcon-like appearance is heightened by the pointed wings and long, rounded tail. The Hawk Owl hunts prey mostly in the daytime and may often be seen hovering somewhat as the Kestrel does. Also reminiscent of the diurnal raptors is its habit of perching with body inclined forward instead of upright as the other owls do.

The mainstay of the Hawk Owl's diet are the small rodents found in its range of distribution in northern Europe, Asia, and North America. Unlike the Snowy Owl, however, it feeds mostly on various kinds of fieldmice and mice (these comprise about 95 per cent of its total intake), hunting lemmings only occasionally. A very agile flier, it also captures birds on the wing.

The three to four eggs are laid in April to June in a shallow depression in the ground. In years when food is very plentiful the clutch may comprise as many as thirteen eggs. Because the female begins incubating as soon as the first egg is laid, there is a marked difference in size between the young. The exact length of incubation and of the period the young spend in the nest before fledging is not known.

FLIGHT SILHOUETTES OF RAPTORS

1 European Black Vulture   *Aegypius monachus*

2 Griffon Vulture   *Gyps fulvus*

3 Lammergeier   *Gypaetus barbatus*

4 Egyptian Vulture   *Neophron percnopterus*

5 Osprey   *Pandion haliaetus*

6 White-tailed or Sea Eagle   *Haliaeetus albicilla*

7 Pallas' Sea Eagle   *Haliaeetus leucoryphus*

1   Golden Eagle   *Aquila chrysaetos*

2   Lesser Spotted Eagle   *Aquila pomarina*

3   Imperial Eagle   *Aquila heliaca*

4   Spotted Eagle   *Aquila clanga*

5   Steppe Eagle   *Aquila rapax nipalensis*

6   Booted Eagle   *Hieraaetus pennatus*

7   Bonelli's Eagle   *Hieraaetus fasciatus*

8   Short-toed Eagle   *Circaetus gallicus*

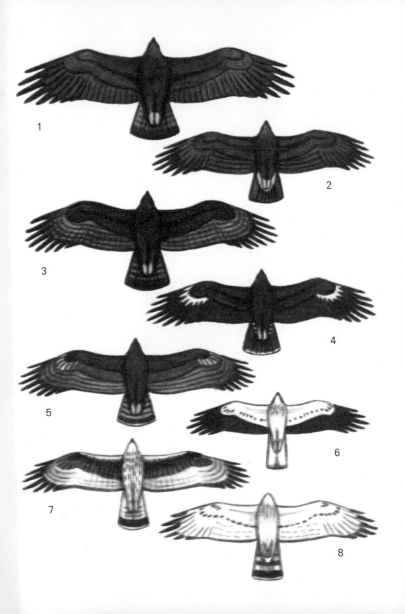

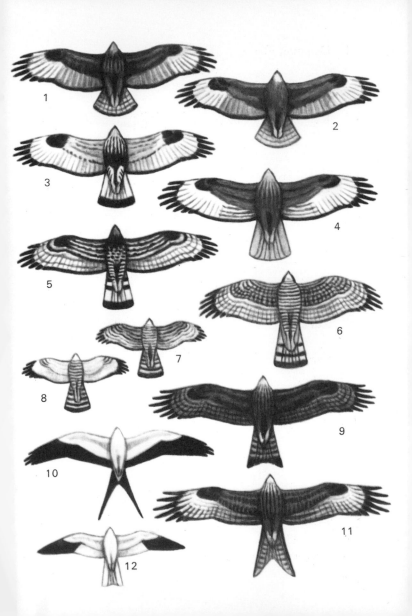

1   Marsh Harrier   *Circus aeruginosus,* male

2   Montagu's Harrier   *Circus pygargus,* male

3   Montagu's Harrier   *Circus pygargus,* young

4   Hen Harrier   *Circus cyaneus,* male

5   Pallid Harrier   *Circus macrourus,* male

6   Kestrel   *Falco tinnunculus,* male

7   Lesser Kestrel   *Falco naumanni,* male

8   Hobby   *Falco subbuteo*

9   Red-footed Falcon   *Falco vespertinus,* male

10   Merlin   *Falco columbarius,* male

11   Eleonora's Falcon   *Falco eleonorae,* light form

12   Gyrfalcon   *Falco rusticolus*

13   White Gyrfalcon   *Falco rusticolus candicans*

14   Peregrine Falcon   *Falco peregrinus*

15   Saker Falcon   *Falco cherrug*

16   Lanner Falcon   *Falco biarmicus*

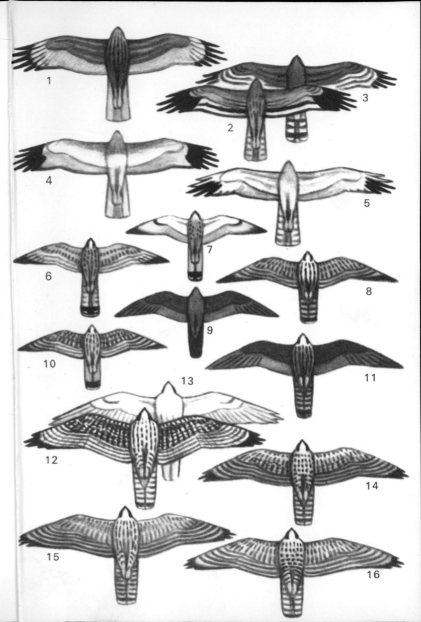

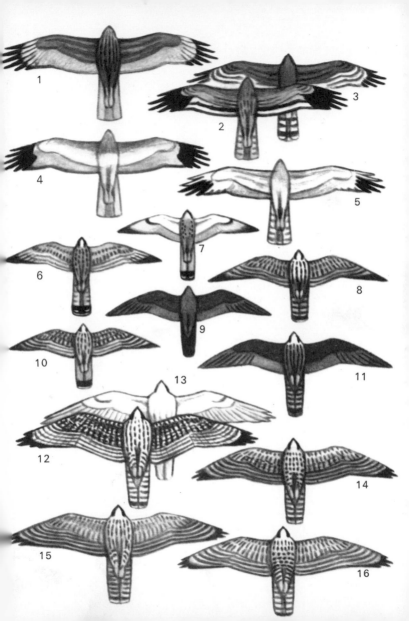

INDEX OF COMMON NAMES

INDEX OF LATIN NAMES